COLLEEN –

COLLIDE !

WHEN YOUR DESIRES
MEET GOD'S HEART

BEN DAILEY

FOREWORD BY TOMMY BARNETT

InfluenceResources.com

Copyright © 2012 by Ben Dailey
ALL RIGHTS RESERVED.

Published by Influence Resources
1455 N. Booneville Ave., Springfield, Missouri 65802

Published in association with The Quadrivium Group—
Orlando, Florida
info@TheQuadriviumGroup.com

Cover concept by Church Media Group, Dallas, Texas. Interior
formatting by Anne McLaughlin, Blue Lake Design, Dickinson, Texas.

Unless otherwise specified, Scripture quotations are taken from the
Holy Bible, New International Version.® Copyright © 1973, 1978, 1984
Biblica. Used by permission of Zondervan. All rights reserved.

Scripture taken from The Message. Copyright © 1993, 1994, 1995,
1996, 2000, 2001, 2002. Used by permission of NavPress Publishing
Group.

The King James Version of the Bible is in the public domain.

Note: All the stories in this book are true, but in a few cases, names
and details have been changed to protect anonymity.

ISBN 978-1-93783-049-6
First printing 2012

Printed in the United States of America

WHAT PEOPLE ARE SAYING ABOUT *COLLIDE* . . .

Ben Dailey is one of the great young leaders of today. In *Collide*, his insights help people navigate the difficult waters of life. I highly recommend this book to those that want to live life instead of drifting sideways. Ben's book helps all of us move forward.
— **Benny Perez, Lead Pastor, The Church, Las Vegas, Nevada, www.thechurchlv.com**

Ben Dailey is an innovative brainiac in this generation. In *Collide* Ben calls you to reconsider if your path is in concert with God's plan. If not, God promises a head-on collision to redirect you to find His plan for your life. You will grow after reading this book!
— **Charles Jenkins, Senior Pastor, Fellowship Church, Chicago, Illinois, www.FellowshipChicago.com**

Ben Dailey speaks brilliantly and intuitively to the heart of one of life's greatest challenges: How do we respond when our desires collide with God's heart? This book will align your perspective, opinion and purpose so you can live the life you were meant to live!
— **Sergio De La Mora, Senior Pastor, Cornerstone Church San Diego, author of**
The Heart Revolution

Difficulties, set backs, and disappointments threatened to derail us, but quite often, these are God's ways of getting our attention. When God's heart collides with our cherished dreams and desires, we have a choice: Will we dive deep into the grace and purposes of God like never before, or will we bail out? In *Collide*, Ben Dailey provides rich spiritual insights and practical suggestions for making these collisions into stepping stones of great growth. I recommend *Collide* to anyone who is serious about walking with Jesus.
— **Ron Carpenter, Senior Pastor, Redemption World Outreach Center, Greenville, South Carolina, author of _The Necessity of the Enemy_**

Collide! People often get hurt in a collision. They didn't see it coming, and their plans change immediately. Some collisions threaten to destroy us. However, colliding with God is different. In love, He collides with you, yet He reaches out to keep you from falling. These collisions aren't a surprise to God. He sees them coming. In fact, they're part of His divine plan. In the middle of the collision, He communicates clearly, "I love you! I want you! I'm with you!" Pastor Ben Dailey unpacks those profound truths with great pragmatism in his book, *Collide*. Fasten your seatbelt as you read this book. You're about to have a collision!
— **Dr. Samuel R. Chand, author of _Cracking Your Church's Culture Code_, www.samchand.com**

CRASH! It happens to us all. In fact, it's inevitable! Ego-driven and intoxicated by narcissism, we drive down the brightly lit but well-worn road of self-serving schemes veiled as dreams when an unexpected collision happens! But don't despair. God has you right where He wants you. My friend Ben Dailey is an agent from Heaven sent to help repair, renew and redirect you from mayhem to magnificence! You're about to be re-routed to true significance.

Ben, thank you for boldly taking this vital subject head-on with a heart of compassion! Joel Osteen and I count it a great privilege to have you as a part of the Champion Network. You represent a new breed of leaders who are relevant and offer great revelation.
— **Phil Munsey, Pastor, Life Church, Irvine, California, Chairman of Champion Network, Lakewood Church/Joel Osteen Ministries**

When Ben Dailey speaks, he draws you into his world. In *Collide*, he describes his own powerful encounters with the heart of God, and he encourages us to face our own collisions with God with faith and hope. I never wonder why Ben Dailey is doing what he's doing. At every point, I know he's had another collision with God.
— **Rich Wilkerson, Pastor, Trinity Church, Miami, Florida**

Ben Dailey is a practitioner who doesn't sit in an ivory tower telling people how to live. He ministers on the ground level where people experience real-life collisions—not just collisions with other people, but collisions with ourselves, our desires, and our God. Ben's book will help everyone who has authentically cried out to God about their purpose, their pain, and their problems. Much grace and "gracism" is needed when our lives experience tension at the intersections between our wants and God's heart. Ben Dailey is a good coach to help the reader at every turn.
— **Dr. David Anderson, Senior Pastor, Bridgeway Community Church Columbia, Maryland, author of *Gracism***

There is a time in every life when our desires and plans collide with God's purpose. This moment always produces a crucial turning point—and the choice we make at this crossroads will determine the course of our lives. In *Collide*, Ben Dailey takes an in-depth look at the amazing, unconditional love of God. God often collides with our desires to redirect us and position us to fulfill our unique, divine purpose. As a young man, Ben Dailey's personal, life-altering encounter with God has given him unique insight into this struggle each Christian faces, and his experience has made him a compassionate pastor and constant friend. I am blessed by Ben's friendship. His character, his experiences and his devoted walk have shaped this book into a valuable resource for anyone searching for God's purpose. If you want to align your dreams with God's heart, this book is for you!
— **Dr. Dave Martin, America's #1 Christian Success Coach, author of *Twelve Traits of the Greats***

Ben Dailey has written a book that is a must-read for those who are serious about God's plan for their lives. With incredible clarity and amazing sensitivity, Ben addresses a dilemma that is a reality of the human experience: What do I do when my agenda and God's will collide? As you read Ben's book, prepare to be captured by the very heart of Jesus and His purpose for your life. You are on a collision course with an incredible, life-changing revelation that addresses real questions and is chock full of real answers!
— Jim Raley, author and Lead Pastor, Calvary Christian Center, Ormond Beach, Florida

Pastor Ben Dailey is a great man of God, pastor, and author. Many people are in need of a collision with God. Some people have already had a collision with Him and need help understanding the next steps. Ben describes our collisions with God and unpacks the steps we need to take. His book *Collide* will transform your thinking, your heart, and your life!
— Herbert Cooper, Senior Pastor, www.peopleschurch.tv

Ben Dailey's new book is a "must-read" for all truth-seekers. Ben writes the way he talks—with relevance, clarity and passion. This book will challenge you, and it will make demands on you. Ben will confront you with the truth of God's love and power in a new, fresh way. By the time you get to the final page, you will sense that you have truly been enlightened. Buckle you seatbelt and get ready for a ride. It will be exciting!
— J. Don George, Founding Pastor, Calvary Church, Irving, Texas

To Kim . . . for being my strongest supporter and best friend. You have stood with me in every season of life—even though I've often been the biggest collision for you! I love you.

To Kyla and Kade . . . for being unbelievable sources of joy in my life. Your love for the Lord has made me the happiest and proudest dad. Through every transition in life you both have walked with tenacity and grace beyond your young years.

CONTENTS

col•lide

To come together with violent, direct impact.

To meet in opposition; conflict.

ACKNOWLEDGEMENTS

God has used many different people to profoundly shape my life and my life's message. Without them, this book wouldn't exist. And without them, my life wouldn't be as rich, full, and meaningful. I want to thank . . .

—My parents, Tim and Laurie Dailey. Your love for me and for Jesus provided the firm foundation of my life. The example you both have set has given me strength through every season of my life.

—Kim's parents, Mike and Randee Ward. You gave me an incredible gift in your daughter. She is a shining legacy of your love for her.

—My brothers: Aaron, Josh, Isaac, Caleb, and Micah. You have been oil and sandpaper in my life. God has used you to fuel me and shape me. You're not only my brothers . . . you're my friends.

—Pastor Don George. You have been a spiritual father to me. You believed in me even when I didn't see potential in myself. I stand on your broad shoulders.

—The Calvary Church staff and servant leaders. What fantastic partners! Your love for God inspires me, and your compassion for hurting people challenges me. It's an honor to serve with you.

—Dr. Sam Chand. At a critical time in my life, you stepped in to encourage me to keep following God. You taught me that true leadership always involves pain tolerance.

—Pat Springle. God used you to draw out the principles of this book and help craft its message.

—Tom Alder. God brought you into my life during a critical season. You reiterated God's purpose for me and encouraged me to press into the future God had spread out before me.

—Steve and Susan Blount. You both believed in a story that I never imagined anyone would care about. You stirred in me excitement and hope that somehow, some way God would use my story.

The love, insights, passion, and courage of these people are found on every page of this book. Because of them, I'm confident God will use it to touch people's lives.

FOREWORD

I met Ben Dailey seventeen years ago when Pastor Don George brought him to our Pastors and Leaders School in Phoenix. From the moment I met him, I was impressed with his honesty, warmth, integrity, and genuine compassion for people. In Ben's eyes, the lost, outcasts, and hurting people don't get in they way of a church's real ministry—they aren't annoyances—they are the reason the church exists. "The least of these" are on God's heart, and they're on Ben's heart, too.

I highly recommend Ben's book to everyone! All of us have a tendency to resist God's gracious will . . . it's easy to drift away from a simple and pure devotion to Christ. Sooner or later, God gets our attention. That's a pleasant way to describe the collision of God's heart and ours. And He always wins! In this book, you'll be challenged to be honest about the pride and apathy in your own heart, but you won't be left in despair. Ben's life and his words bring us back to the cross of Christ where we find forgiveness, restoration, and a new hope for the future.

When God's heart collides with ours, everything changes. God transforms our direction, our passions, and our relationships. We care about the people God cares for, our hearts break over the things that break His heart, and we live for His honor and glory. Some people think they can wear the mask of "a nice Christian" to impress people, but this mask eventually falls away. We need more than a mask—far more. We need the work of the Holy Spirit to shine His light into the recesses of our hearts, and we need Him to radically change us from the inside out.

One of the measuring sticks of a changed heart is our love for others—especially enemies, foreigners, gross sinners, outcasts, and those who can give us nothing in return. These are the people who flocked to Jesus because they sensed His genuine love for them. Ben's church is a place like that.

The prophet Micah described the new heart God puts in us:

> O people, the Lord has told you what is good,
>   and this is what he requires of you:
> to do what is right, to love mercy,
>   and to walk humbly with your God (Micah 6:8).

Doing right, mercy, and humility—that's what Ben's book is about. God has anointed him with power and grace. People in his community sense the love of God pouring from the people who go to Calvary Church, and it's changing their lives.

I'm so proud of Ben Dailey. I've watched him grow as a man, a husband, a father, a teacher, and a leader. God has broken his heart and filled it with His strength and love. When you read this book, be open to the Spirit's whisper, nudge, and shout. A collision is coming. You can count on it.

Tommy Barnett

Senior Pastor of Phoenix First Assembly of God,
"The Church with a Heart"

Co-Pastor of the Los Angeles Dream Center,
"The Church that Never Sleeps"

Chancellor of Southeastern University

CHAPTER 1
CATCHING GOD'S HEART

We should be astonished at the goodness of
God, stunned that He should bother to call us
by name, our mouths wide open at His love,
bewildered that at this very moment we are
standing on holy ground.

—Brennan Manning

It's inevitable. Sooner or later, our desires collide with God's heart. His
purposes are far higher than ours, His wisdom far deeper, and His love
far wider. From our limited perspective, we think we know what God
should do to bless us. We have dreams for our careers, our marriages,
our kids, and every other aspect of life.

Sometimes we're right on track, but today, tomorrow, or a year from
now, we might realize our hopes and dreams have crashed. When that
happens, we have a decision to make: Will we shake our fist at God and
walk away, or cling to Him more tenaciously than ever before? The moment our desires collide with God may seem like the end of a dream, but
in reality, it's the beginning of fresh insights and renewed hope.

Sometimes we welcome such collisions, but quite often, they shatter us into pieces.

THE SHED

By the time I was 18, I had drifted away from God, the church, and the Christian life. For years, I watched my mom and dad fulfill the two greatest commandments (Matthew 22:34-40) more than any human beings I'd ever known. My dad was (and is) a pastor. He and my mother loved God with all their hearts, and they loved people without preconditions. During my childhood, I saw them lead worship with passion and power, and they were incredibly generous. Our family didn't have much in material wealth, but my parents shared what they had with anyone in need. We had an apartment in our home, and someone always lived in it. My mom and dad welcomed addicts, single moms, people whose marriages were in shambles, some who struggled with depression, and anyone else who needed a roof, some good food, and the warmth of a loving family.

Mom and Dad weren't trying to impress anyone, and they didn't reach out because they were pressured by guilt. The love of God had been poured into their hearts, and it overflowed into the lives of people in need. It's as simple and marvelous as that. They were amazing.

My departure from the faith was in response to verbal attacks my parents suffered. As they pursued the fullness of the Spirit, pastors in their fellowship of independent churches severely criticized them. My mom and dad had promised to avoid causing a church split, so Dad resigned as the pastor. It was shocking, but true. After my parents left, they continued to invite hurting people to live with us, but they no longer had financial support.

Sometimes when I got up in the morning, I saw my mom sitting under the covers on her bed, praying for the outcasts she and Dad had brought under their roof. I remember Dad gathering Mom and my brothers, six boys in all, together. He said, "I need you to know that the last food in the house will run out today, but don't despair. We're going to trust God to provide." He had a smile on his face. He wasn't bitter, and he wasn't worried. (At least that's how it appeared to us.) He trusted the King of the universe to provide. The next morning, sacks of groceries appeared at the front door like manna from heaven. My mom and dad were the most loving, giving people I'd ever known, but they had become outcasts. Even after church leaders had viciously attacked them, I never heard them utter an unkind word in return.

The more I looked at the situation, the more I concluded, "This whole thing sucks!" How could God let two of His most devoted children suffer so much?

The more I looked at the situation, the more I concluded, "This whole thing sucks!" How could God let two of His most devoted children suffer so much? I admired my parents more than ever, but they were getting a raw deal. It wasn't fair. I waited a long time for God to fix the situation, but He didn't do it the way I thought He should have. When God seemed to give up on my mom and dad, I gave up on Him. I didn't hate God, but I was sure He was giving my parents the short end of the stick.

I know a lot of people who look back at the relationship with their parents and cringe. They felt abandoned, controlled, or criticized. That was not my experience in the least. My parents loved me—even more than they loved the down-and-out people they welcomed into our home. I never felt neglected.

Nor was I ever pressured to become a pastor like my dad. He often said, "Son, you can become anything you want to be; just love Jesus with all your heart." My adolescent angst wasn't the normal teenage rebellion against authority. In fact, I didn't want anything I did or said to ever dishonor my parents—especially my dad. I never wanted to give our critics in the church more ammunition to use against him.

Even though I was terribly frustrated with God and the church leaders who were hurting my parents, I continued to go to my dad's church. At the time, my perception of church people other than my parents was that they were backward, angry, and poor. I didn't want to have anything to do with them. When people asked me what my dad did, I told them, "He's a motivational speaker." I didn't want to be branded as a preacher's kid. My lie was pointless, however, because everybody in our little town knew my dad—personally or by reputation. (Ironically, I now sometimes introduce myself as a motivational speaker.)

Our family lived on the coast of central California. When I graduated from high school, I wanted to go to college—but not just anywhere. I felt drawn to the bright lights of Los Angeles where I could make a name for myself and live large. Days before I planned to leave home, I had a radical collision with God.

The summer before my senior year, my parents moved to a town about 45 minutes away. I didn't want to start over with new friends for my last year in school, so I stayed in our hometown for my final year. Then, after graduation, I moved to live with my mom and dad. My father had converted a shed in the backyard into a bedroom for me. All summer, I lived in the shed.

On the night of August 8, I went to bed with nothing special on my mind, but a few hours later, I woke up under the fierce conviction of the Holy Spirit. I had felt the Spirit point out sin in my life before—plenty of times. But this was different. The experience was far more vivid, more intense, and more penetrating than anything I'd ever felt. The light of God shined into the crevices of my heart and revealed the darkness. Suddenly, I realized I had been drifting. I cared far more about success, pleasure, approval, and excitement than God's purpose for my life. With blinding clarity, I saw that everything I thought was right was wrong, and everything I thought was wrong was right. My goals in life had become completely absorbed in the world's values. I cared only about myself. Everyone and everything else only had value if they contributed to my success and my reputation. Nothing else mattered. And all my sin stank in God's nostrils.

The light of God shined into the crevices of my heart and revealed the darkness. Suddenly, I realized I had been drifting.

I tried to get away by making excuses, but in the shed that night, God wouldn't let go of me. All night, God reminded me of passages of Scripture I'd heard in my dad's sermons and around the dinner table. Each one stabbed at my heart. For example, in one of the letters to the seven churches in Revelation, Jesus had said:

> "You say, 'I am rich; I have acquired wealth and do not need a thing.' But you do not realize that you are wretched, pitiful, poor, blind and naked. I counsel you to buy from me gold refined in the fire, so you can become rich; and white clothes to wear, so you can cover your shameful nakedness; and salve to put on your eyes, so you can see" (Revelation 3:17-18).

I couldn't deny the Spirit's truthful assessment of my heart. I had become self-absorbed, self-confident, self-sufficient, and every other horrible, hyphenated "self-" word. I thought I had the world by the tail until my desires collided with God's heart that night. I didn't realize I was so "wretched, pitiful, poor, blind, and naked." The only remedy was to clothe myself in the grace of God and experience His forgiveness.

From 11:00 that night until 6:00 the next morning, I wept, wrestled, and cried out to God. Like Jacob, I tried to get the upper hand in the struggle, but it was no use. God's love and power were too much for me. And like Jacob, God allowed me to walk away from my wrestling match with a new awareness of His kindness and mercy. As dawn broke, I finally told Him, "God, you win. I give up. I'll be the person you want me to be, and I'll do the things you want me to do."

Mine was not some bland, blanket confession. God had pointed out specific attitudes, patterns of behavior, and wrong relationships I had cultivated. I knew He wanted me to repent: to change my heart as well as my direction in all those things. God's Spirit dealt with me about the full range of commitments, from my ultimate purpose in life to the words coming out of my mouth each day. Nothing was off limits. God wanted me to change in virtually every way.

Exhausted but relieved, I got off the floor and lay on my bed. At that moment, I had an unmistakable, supernatural encounter with God's Spirit—even more intense and more wonderful than His presence during the night.

My first act of obedience was to get rid of the stuff that had been clouding my perspective and stealing my heart. I had really been into music. I carried out stacks of cassettes, CDs, posters, and magazines—distractions that had taken control of my heart. There was no more denying it; they all had to go.

Was my response too drastic? I don't think so. I needed to respond to God's Spirit with everything in me. I wanted to make a statement to Him and to my own heart that I was serious about following Him. I didn't want to leave the smallest thing that could divert my heart from God. No half measures, no excuses.

That morning I gave my whole heart to the Lord. From that point onward I would go where He led me to go, say what He wanted me to say, and do whatever He wanted me to do. Like a poker player, I was "all in." Don't misunderstand: I'm not suggesting that listening to popular music and reading *Rolling Stone* is evil and sinful for everybody. But those things had become distractions to me, so they had to go. All of us have "stuff" that threatens to distract us. If we want to experience God's best, we need to identify our obstacles and deal with them ruthlessly.

I didn't want to leave the smallest thing that could divert my heart from God. No half measures, no excuses.

By the time my mom got up to cook breakfast, I was hauling piles of stuff out to the trashcan. At one point, I looked toward the house and saw seven faces staring at me. They wondered what in the world I was doing, and they probably thought I'd lost my mind. I walked to the house and told them what had happened all night. I explained, "I don't know where God is leading me. All I know is that I'm going to follow Him wherever He takes me."

I soon had confirmation that God had brought me to a good decision. One of the points of collision during the night was about my relationship with Kim. We had been dating for a long time, but I treated her the way I treated God: I had been taking her for granted. During the night, God showed me that she was the one He had chosen for me to marry. I was thrilled, but there was a problem. Kim had recently taken stock of our relationship and had come to a very different conclusion. She and my mom were very close, and Kim planned to come to the house to tell my mom that she was going to break up with me. Who could blame her? She had only been a Christian for about three years, and I was her example of a follower of Jesus Christ—a *bad* example.

Kim had wrestled with God for a long time about our relationship. She was ready to tell my mom, "I believe God has a call on my life, but I don't think Ben is serious about his walk with Jesus. I want to stay connected with you, but I have to walk away from Ben." But before she came over, God intervened and confirmed that He wanted us to get married. After I told her about my collision with God in the shed, she told me about her collision with God at the exact same time. Just a coincidence? I don't think so. Now it made sense that God wanted us to be together. God was already putting the most important pieces of my life's puzzle into place. Both Kim and I were fully committed to take God's hand and follow Him.

ALL OF US ALL THE TIME

God's invitation isn't just for pastors, evangelists, and missionaries. God's kingdom is not structured with a higher and lower order of roles. All of us are called to know Him, love Him, and follow Him with all our hearts. Martin Luther said that washing dishes was a noble, godly profession if the dishwasher does it to the glory of God. When we catch God's heart (and more importantly, when He captures ours), we want to invest every resource, talent, and moment in pleasing Him. He leads a few people into fulltime ministry, but He leads all of us into fulltime passion to honor Him. I know godly and passionate Christians in all walks of life: plumbers, attorneys, landscapers, salespeople, doctors, and others. God uses us where He places us.

When we catch God's heart (and more importantly, when He captures ours), we want to invest every resource, talent, and moment in pleasing Him.

When William Wilberforce became a Christian, he assumed God would want him to resign as a Member of Parliament and become a pastor. He talked to John Newton, former captain of a slave ship and the author of "Amazing Grace." Newton told Wilberforce he could serve God more effectively in his current role than as a pastor. Wilberforce stayed in Parliament, and God used him as the catalyst to abolish the slave trade in the British Empire. God wants to use each of us in incredible ways to touch the lives of people around us, but first many of us need a collision with God's heart to change our direction.

We can encounter different types of collisions. Initially, we may not recognize how they connect with God. Some occur when we confront difficult people, some arise when a dream dies, and some threaten our stability during a time of calamity. On the surface, it may not appear that our desires are colliding with God's heart, but if we peel down a layer or two, that's exactly what's happening. Every difficulty is a collision between our hidden desires and God's purpose for us.

Sir Isaac Newton was one of the greatest scientists the world has ever known. His three laws of motion revolutionized the study of physics. The first law states: "Every object in a state of uniform motion tends to remain in that state of motion unless an external force is applied to it."

In other words, collisions matter: The greater the force of impact, the greater the change of course.

Newton's principle has a spiritual application as well. Each of us heads in a direction that seems completely right and reasonable, but God is the ultimate external force. When we were headed to eternal destruction, Jesus stepped out of heaven to collide with the human race to change our direction. And He continues to step into the life of every believer so that His love and purpose collide with our desires.

STILL ALL ABOUT ME
After the collision in the shed, Kim and I embarked on a great adventure. We were excited, although we still didn't understand some very important truths about our renewed spiritual life. In the physical world, babies have a "new life," but their whole world revolves around their immediate needs and desires. They don't think about the hopes and dreams of others. The circle of their world is only a dot . . . their own dot. The same is true in a spiritual sense: Young Christians—even those who have had a dramatic encounter with God in a shed—can remain self-focused.

In the months following my night of wrestling with God, my life took on an exciting new trajectory, but I was still thinking primarily about myself. I prayed about what God would do in me, for me, to me, and through me. When I read the Scriptures, I looked for passages that promised God's blessings for me. I was convinced I was "caught up in the jet stream of God's Spirit," and the Christian life would be easy. If God was in it, He would make everything smooth and successful, wouldn't He? I was sure God would bring incredible blessings without any hint of disappointment. He was going to supernaturally blow away any obstacle and shower His blessings on us! Favor and blessing, I was sure, were the inevitable results of God's calling.

I had an important lesson to learn. I had assumed that if God was leading me, life was going to be easy. But I discovered a different truth: Because God was leading me, life wasn't going to be easy at all. There's nothing wrong with praying for God's blessings and asking Him to open doors of opportunity, but I needed to learn that the way of the cross always involves both blessings and suffering. I couldn't have one without the other.

I had assumed that if God was leading me, life was going to be easy. But I discovered a different truth: Because God was leading me, life wasn't going to be easy at all.

When we experience collisions—often in the form of distractions and unexpected disappointments—we tend to respond in several ways:

- We second-guess God's call and our decision to follow Him;

- We get confused about the meaning of spiritual life. (Can walking with God really be this hard?);

- We blame God because "He didn't come through like He promised";

- We engage in morbid introspection, trying to find some hidden sin to blame for the absence of God's blessing; or,

- We can humbly trust that in God's sovereignty and goodness, He has deeper lessons for us to learn. Hardships and disappointments are His classroom.

To be sure, God often pours out His blessings in abundant measure on young Christians. To confirm them in their new faith and give them assurance of their heavenly Father's attentive care, God often gives new believers unusual answers to prayer. Sooner or later, though, He wants all of us to grow beyond spiritual infancy. To deepen our dependence on Him, God takes us through a series of difficulties.

In his outstanding book, *Knowing God,* author and professor J.I. Packer explains,

> This is what all the work of grace aims at—an even deeper knowledge of God, and an ever closer fellowship with Him. Grace is God drawing us sinners closer and closer to Him. How does God in grace prosecute this purpose? Not by shielding us from assault by the world, the flesh, and the devil, nor by protecting us from burdensome and frustrating circumstances, nor yet by shielding us from troubles created by our own temperament and psychology; but rather by exposing us to all these things, so as to overwhelm us with a sense of our own inadequacy, and to drive us to cling to Him more closely. This is the ultimate reason, from our standpoint, why God fills our lives with troubles and perplexities of one sort or another—it is to ensure that we shall learn to hold Him fast.[1]

Many of us read our Bibles and listen to messages about grace, but truth doesn't sink in. We believe we have leverage with God if we follow some list of rules closely enough to earn points with God. When times are good, we think we're being rewarded. But when our desires collide with God's heart, we walk away in confusion or shake our fist

---

1   J.I. Packer, *Knowing God* (Downers Grove: InterVarsity Press, 1973), p. 227.

at God and ask, "God, what's the deal? Look at all I've done for you!" We may not say it, but we secretly want to tell Him, "I deserve better than this!"

Sometimes a person tells me, "Pastor, I don't know what happened. I went to college and got a degree, but all I can find is a dead-end job." Or, "Pastor Ben, I've been a good girl like my mother told me to be. Why hasn't God sent a Prince Charming for me to marry?" A few have told me, "I go to church. I even take notes on the sermon. I tithe (sometimes) and volunteer, but my life's not what I expected it to be. I feel like God has let me down." To compound misery, these people get mad at themselves for having less than perfect joy as they wrestle with their disappointments. They feel stuck on a treadmill of endless effort and deep discouragement—but they assume everybody else is doing great, so they aren't honest about their struggles.

Many of us are like the elder brother in Jesus' story of the prodigal son, who did right things, but for wrong reasons. He worked hard, but not because he delighted in his father's love and wanted to honor him. He labored every day because he wanted to earn his inheritance. He felt superior to his younger brother, and he was furious with his forgiving dad when little brother returned. The human heart drifts toward a toxic blend of self-justification and entitlement—we believe we have to earn God's blessings, and we're sure we deserve them! It takes a humble heart to admit we deserve nothing, yet we've received everything from the open hand of God.

Following God doesn't guarantee immediate success and blessings. We don't have to look far in the Bible to realize this truth. David was anointed King of Israel while a shepherd boy, but he faced the jealousy and rage of Saul for a long while before he assumed the throne.

The prophets in the Old Testament spoke out boldly and courageously, many times at risk of death for telling the truth.

Of course, there has never been anyone who followed the Father's will like Jesus did. He certainly had no easy life. He was ridiculed, rejected, betrayed, tortured, and executed. The apostle Paul had a fateful collision with God on the road to Damascus, and his transformation began a lifetime of suffering for his Lord. Near the end of his life, he was warned of personal danger awaiting him in Jerusalem. Instead of taking the easy way out, Paul told them:

> And now, compelled by the Spirit, I am going to Jerusalem, not knowing what will happen to me there. I only know that in every city the Holy Spirit warns me that prison and hardships are facing me. However, I consider my life worth nothing to me; my only aim is to finish the race and complete the task the Lord Jesus has given me—the task of testifying to the good news of God's grace (Acts 20:22-24).

It helps to understand the difference between being *called* and being *chosen*. Every person who says "Yes" to Christ's offer of forgiveness and eternal life is called by God to be His beloved child. It's a free gift and the highest honor we can ever know. Then, at some point, our desires collide with God, and we realize life is about much more than ourselves. At that moment God chooses us to walk with Him in a deeper relationship. To take those next steps, we have to abandon the infantile expectations of the past and embrace the more difficult process that leads to spiritual maturity. We choose to take God's hand and walk with Him wherever He leads, whether the journey is pleasant, confusing, or excruciatingly painful. When we realize we are *chosen* by God, we don't compare our circumstances and our journey with anyone else's. We aren't jealous and we aren't disappointed. We realize His plan for us has been uniquely and divinely crafted—full of blessings and heartaches—to fulfill His purposes, not ours.

A GLIMPSE INTO GOD'S HEART

In our culture, fathers are an endangered species. The breakdown of the family is measured in statistics about the divorce rate, mobility, addictions, and distractions, but those numbers can't describe the damage in the hearts of every person involved. Even among intact families, fathers are often preoccupied with work, or they feel condemned for falling short so often at home. They may sleep under the same roof as the wife and kids, but emotionally, they've checked out.

I see many people in our church and our community who have grown up without a dad. God has constructed the family for fathers to provide a powerful blend of affection, protection, and provision. When those qualities are diminished, the souls of the wife and kids are impoverished. (There's much more on this in a later chapter.) I'm not trying to rag on fathers. I'm only showing that the concept of our heavenly Father is often adversely shaped by the relationship—or lack of relationship—with our earthy dads.

We realize His plan for us has been uniquely and divinely crafted—full of blessings and heartaches—to fulfill His purposes, not ours.

Who can blame people for needing help to get a glimpse of God's heart? The disciples had spent more than three years in the physical presence of Jesus. Every day—on hillsides, in towns, on the sea, among tombs, and on the roads—they had seen Him loving, protecting, and providing for people. He healed lepers, raised the dead, cast out demons, refuted angry Pharisees, welcomed outcasts, and shared His heart with countless people. But on the night He was hosting the twelve disciples one last time, Jesus again told them He was going to die—and soon. Thomas was confused. He asked, "Where are you going? How will we know the way?"

Jesus replied, "I am the way and the truth and the life. No one comes to the Father except through me. If you really know me, you will know my Father as well. From now on, you do know him and have seen him" (John 14:6-7).

Philip still didn't get it. He asked Jesus for a sign: "Lord, show us the Father and that will be enough for us."

No one would have blamed Jesus if, at that moment, He'd thrown up His hands and walked off. But instead, He patiently explained, "Don't you know me, Philip, even after I have been among you such a long time? Anyone who has seen me has seen the Father. How can you say, 'Show us the Father'? Don't you believe that I am in the Father, and that the Father is in me? The words I say to you I do not speak on my own authority. Rather, it is the Father, living in me, who is doing his work" (John 14:9-10).

How do we know what the Father is like? By looking at the life of Jesus. Misconceptions come in all shapes and sizes. We may think of God as a harsh judge, a cop waiting to catch us doing something wrong, a Santa Claus who is kind but not very sharp, a negotiator we can bargain with until we get a good deal,

How do we know what the Father is like?

By looking at the life of Jesus.

or a distant "stained-glass guy" who looks nice but can't really relate to our hopes and dreams. But God isn't like any of those misconceptions.

In an article written long ago, B.B. Warfield described "The Emotional Life of Our Lord."[2] He studied every mention of Christ's emotions in the Gospels, and he found one that was mentioned more than all the others combined: *compassion*. We sometimes think of compassion as "kind intention." The Gospel writers meant more than that. The word actually means, "to have trembling bowels." In other words, biblical compassion is such a deep degree of care that it gnaws at your gut. Jesus cared that much for people who were lost, those who were hurting, and even for the rich young man who walked away from Him.

The love of God is never weak and wimpy. God is the creator of the universe—the one who spoke and 200 billion galaxies were flung into space. His power is far greater than anything we can imagine, and it's matched by His infinite wisdom. The Bible says He uses the earth as His ottoman to prop up His feet. He counts the hairs on our heads, and He controls the electrons in the stars in the most distant galaxy. He provides a limitless supply of love, power, and wisdom.

What difference does this make? Two events give us a picture of God's heart: creation and the cross. The vast expanse of creation displays God's magnificent greatness; Christ's willing sacrifice on the cross shouts of His extravagant love. When we are amazed at His greatness and grace, everything changes. Our worship becomes more passionate, our obedience more joyful, our giving more lavish, and our prayers more focused on praise than requests. In the absence of delight, we

---

2   B. B. Warfield, "The Emotional Life of Our Lord," cited on
     3/19/12 at www.the-highway.com/emotion-Christ_Warfield.html

think of God as a tool by which we accomplish our goals. But when our hearts are filled with wonder, we find Him beautiful. All earthly fathers, even the best of them, are flawed and limited (just ask my kids), but our heavenly Father has proven Himself beyond all doubt. This perspective changes how we think about the collision between our desires and God's heart.

HEART'S DESIRES

When Christians talk about their desires, they often quote Psalm 37:4: "Take delight in the Lord, and he will give you the desires of your heart." But many believers totally misunderstand this verse. They see it as a guarantee that God will give them whatever they want. That's not it at all! The passage begins with a condition: "Take delight in the Lord." The first item of business, then, isn't getting what we want; it's putting our hearts in the right place.

When our hearts are in alignment with God—when we're amazed at the wonder of His love, power, protection, and provision—He changes us from the inside out. In a very real sense, we get a heart transplant. Gradually, we want what God wants, we care about the people He loves, and our hearts break over the same things that break His heart.

When our hearts are in alignment with God—when we're amazed at the wonder of His love, power, protection, and provision—He changes us from the inside out.

The alternative to taking delight in God is to go in the opposite direction. Some people are well aware of the darkness in their hearts, but they don't believe they can ever have good and godly desires. They settle for a second-class experience with God, and many completely give up on God.

The greatest delight isn't the blessings God gives us. Don't get me wrong. I'm always down for God's blessings in my life. Bring 'em on! They're wonderful, but there is something far better: knowing, loving, and delighting in God Himself. Most people, even those who sit in the pews every Sunday morning, have come to believe that the Christian experience is only a bunch of rules and empty promises, so they pursue other things to fill up their hearts. They pursue success, pleasure, prestige, possessions, and approval. For a short time, such counterfeits seem to fill the void, but not for long.

Augustine said only one thing can fill the gaping hole in our hearts. In his *Confessions*, he prayed, "You have made us for yourself, O God, and our hearts are restless until they find their rest in you."[3] All the counterfeits may promise a rich and meaningful life, but they ultimately fail.

Throughout the ages, some philosophers and religious leaders advised people to get rid of their desires. The solution, they suggested, was to become numb to the deep drives of the human heart. Desire, though, isn't evil. In fact, the great people of the Bible and history have been passionate people. The problem isn't that we desire too much, but that we set our sights too low. In *Mere Christianity*, C.S. Lewis noted,

> We are half-hearted creatures, fooling around with drink and sex, and ambition, when infinite joy is offered us, like an ignorant child who wants to go on making mud pies in a slum

---

3   St. Augustine, *Confessions* (Oxford: Oxford University Press, 2009), p. 1.

because he cannot imagine what is meant by the offer of a holiday at the sea. We are far too easily pleased.[4]

We can do better than mud pies.

SIGNS

How can we tell when we've collided with God's heart? There are many signs: We increasingly delight in God, love unlovely people, give to those who can't pay us back, and serve without demanding anything in return.

How can we tell when we've collided with God's heart? There are many signs: We increasingly delight in God, love unlovely people, give to those who can't pay us back, and serve without demanding anything in return.

To *delight* means "to derive pleasure" from someone or something. When we delight in God, it's not drudgery. Instead of dreading prayer, Bible study, worship, and service, we can't wait to get to hang out with the One we love! The Scriptures compare our relationship with God to marriage. He's the groom, and we're His beloved bride. A strong marriage is secure and intimate, and it produces offspring. In the same way, when we delight in God, our joy in knowing Him spills out in conversations with others, and many of them want to know Him, too. Affection and wonder are so powerful they can't be contained. They overflow from us. One of God's promises is that we'll live with Him for

---

4   C.S. Lewis, *Mere Christianity* (San Francisco: HarperSanFrancisco, 2001), p. 50.

eternity. Why so long? Because it will take that long to explore God's infinite love, power, and wisdom.

Heart change doesn't happen by magic, and it doesn't occur by osmosis as we sit in church an hour a week (if that!). It requires focused attention. We can't know God's heart unless we spend time with Him. We learn to delight in Him by reading the Scriptures to see His beauty, and our delight deepens as we connect with Him in prayer. But delighting in God isn't just a private matter. Corporate worship enables us to have a bigger view of God and His work in people's lives, and reaching out to care for others lets us become His hands, feet, and voice.

Following a set of religious rules never produces true delight and glad obedience. Rules (without a relationship) only create a sense of empty obligation, resentment, and anger. Responding to the wonder of God's love delights both Him and us. Like two lovers, we enjoy pleasing each other, and nothing is off limits for discussion.

During the conversation between Jesus, Thomas, and Philip about knowing the Father, Jesus explained that when we're in tune with the Father's heart, we can pray bold prayers: "And I will do whatever you ask in my name, so that the Father may be glorified in the Son. You may ask me for anything in my name, and I will do it" (John 14:13-14). Jesus isn't promising a blank check to fulfill our selfish desires. Instead, He promises that if our hearts belong to God, we will want what He wants, so our prayers will be in line with His purposes. When we pray this way, God loves to answer us. When He answers, we pray even more confidently . . . and the dance continues.

THE FIGHT

The message of the gospel is that Jesus Christ stepped out of the glory of heaven to take on human flesh so He could pay the ultimate price for you and me. Even in this monumental sacrifice, He didn't pay it and walk away. He longs for a rich, intimate relationship with us. He pursues us and engages us. It's astounding: Almighty God wants a relationship with puny, selfish, terribly flawed people like us! He doesn't demand that we clean up our act before He reaches out to touch our hearts. He reaches out *in spite of* our selfishness and pride. That's what grace is all about. But knowing Him never leaves us the same. When the kindness of God leads us to repentance (Romans 2:4), He begins to change our "have to's" into "want to's."

When the kindness of God leads us to repentance (Romans 2:4), He begins to change our "have to's" into "want to's."

In our culture, love almost always comes with strings attached. People appreciate us *if* we make them happy. They pay attention to us *when* we contribute to their success. In business and neighborhoods, the measuring sticks are bank accounts, cars, clothes, vacations, and titles. In the church, we have our own set of measuring sticks to see if we're "one up" on those around us: attendance, service, giving, exuberance in worship, and many others. Again, there's nothing wrong with those things if they come from a heart full of God's love, but there's everything wrong with them when we use them to feel superior to others or attempt to twist God's arm to get Him to bless us.

God offers His grace fully and freely. He doesn't love us "if" we pray, read the Bible, go to church, give, or serve. Just the opposite. He loved us "when we were yet sinners" (Romans 5:8), when we had nothing to offer Him. Left to itself, the human heart runs on doubt and rules. It's a fight to change our view of God from one of the misconceptions (judge, cop, Santa Claus, negotiator, or "stained glass guy") to the way He is presented in Scripture. We fight an internal war to fully believe that God's grace is true, right, and real.

Jesus told a story about two men who went to the temple to pray (Luke 18:9-14). One of them was a hated tax collector. He was so stricken with his sin that he couldn't even look up to heaven. In sorrow and guilt, he beat his breast and pled, "God, have mercy on me, a sinner!" The other man was a religious person who followed all the rules. When he prayed, he reminded God how much he had done for Him, and when he saw the tax collector, he remarked, "And I'm sure glad I'm not like that guy!" Jesus said only one of the two went away with a clean heart: the tax collector.

Which one is more like you? Are you so aware of your flaws that you humble yourself before God and know that only His grace can save you? Or are you counting on all your religious deeds to earn points with God?

If we believe God's love comes with conditions, we'll follow Him only if we think we're getting a good deal. When we don't delight in God, every difficulty seems like a prison. But as we learn to delight in God, we trust Him even when life makes no sense, when things don't work out the way we hoped, when our prayers remain unanswered, and when our dreams die. Our hearts are filled with wonder at His love and grace, and our problems become classrooms to teach us life's most important lessons.

A familiar passage in Proverbs states:

> Trust in the Lord with all your heart
>> and lean not on your own understanding;
> in all your ways submit to him,
>> and he will make your paths straight (Proverbs 3:5-6).

Note the two courses for our lives: We can trust God with all our hearts, or we can lean on our own understanding. If we delight in God and trust that He is infinitely wise, kind, good, and powerful—even when we don't see His hand at work—we can be confident that He will guide our steps and accomplish His purposes in our lives. But if we trust our ability to figure things out and make life work, we'll endure needless frustration, emptiness, heartache, and confusion.

Trust isn't something we conjure up at the spur of the moment. It's the product of thinking, considering, and grasping the nature of God's heart for us.

Trust isn't something we conjure up at the spur of the moment. It's the product of thinking, considering, and grasping the nature of God's heart for us. When we know the love of Christ that surpasses knowledge (Ephesians 3:19), we will trust Him even in darkness and difficulty. When our hearts connect with God's, we can face anything. Oh, we hurt, we grieve, and we experience the full range of emotions, but underneath it all, we have a bedrock of confidence in God.

At the close of Paul's beautiful and powerful chapter on the grace of God in his letter to the Romans, he wrote:

Who shall separate us from the love of Christ? Shall trouble
or hardship or persecution or famine or nakedness or danger
or sword? . . . For I am convinced that neither death nor life,
neither angels nor demons, neither the present nor the future, nor any powers, neither height nor depth, nor anything
else in all creation, will be able to separate us from the love
of God that is in Christ Jesus our Lord (Romans 8:35, 38-39).

I sure don't want to give the impression that "I've arrived." God has
worked deeply in me to show me more of His love, but I still have a long
way to go. More than ever, I realize that merely following rules doesn't
cut it, and demanding that God jump through hoops poisons my relationship with Him. Looking at the disciples gives me encouragement. I
used to think they were a bunch of losers because they were so slow to
understand Christ's character and purpose, but then I realized I'm just
like them: just as slow, just as dense, and just as desperately in need of
Jesus' patience and compassion.

I hope you have lots of people encouraging you to be honest about
your sins and your misconceptions about God so you can be refreshed
by His grace. I want this book to be one more voice to invite you to go
deeper in your experience of His heart.

You may have been a Christian for years, but now realize you've been
a Pharisee. It's time to delight in God's grace.

You may be a new believer who is thrilled to find the love of God. Don't
settle for a superficial relationship, and don't let your faith slip into
empty rules. Stay fresh with the love and tenderness of God.

You may be someone who is still seeking the truth about Jesus. Open
your heart to God's magnificent, unconditional love.

God isn't impressed by all you might try to do for Him. He's looking for people who are honest about their darkest sins and deepest needs, and He loves to shower His grace on them! For all of us, delighting in God's heart is a process—one that necessarily involves mountaintops and valleys. Don't be shocked when you find yourself in one of the valleys. That's where we learn to lean on God more than ever.

The Bible speaks of three tenses of salvation. When we trusted in Christ, we *were saved*. As we trust Him each day and experience His transforming power, we *are being saved*. And one day, we *will be saved* and enjoy the consummation of His grace in the New Heaven and New Earth. On that day, we will have resurrected bodies, freedom from the presence of sin, and a face-to-face relationship with God.

The Lord didn't rescue us from sin and push us out on our own. Today and tomorrow and every day, He is with us, He cares, and we can trust Him. Each day, we catch a little more of His heart. God loves us enough to collide with our desires—not to punish us, but to push us, prod us, and invite us to experience His presence, purpose, and power. When my desires collided with God's heart in the shed behind my parents' house, it initially felt like my world was coming to an end, but then I realized it was the beginning.

At the end of each chapter, you'll find a few questions to help you apply the principles we've covered. The goal isn't to fill in the blanks. Take your time, and invite the Spirit of God to connect with your heart. Let His truth simmer in your thoughts, and be open to His voice.

THINK ABOUT IT...

1. What does it mean to "catch God's heart"?

2. Which of the misconceptions of the character of God (judge, cop, etc.) have you experienced? How did it affect your understanding of His grace and love? What has helped you perceive God more accurately?

3. Why is it crucial to delight in God? What helps you enjoy Him and be amazed at Him?

4. How does delighting in God change our desires?

5. Why is it so hard to have a humble, thankful, wonder-filled heart instead of trusting in our ability to impress God by following rules? How are you doing in this fight?

6. Are collisions with God's heart good things or bad things? Explain your answer.

CHAPTER 2
HEART ATTACKS

We view things not only from different sides
but with different eyes.

—Blaise Pascal

Things aren't always what they seem. In the movie *Vantage Point*, we see the apparent assassination of the President of the United States through the eyes of eight people. As the story unfolds, we get glimpses of terrorism, complex plots, murder, and love. With each new perspective, we get a little closer to discovering the real truth, but no one knows the full picture until the very end.

The movie is a metaphor for how we often fail to see the whole picture in our lives. We think we see things perfectly, so we assume we know exactly how life should go. Sooner or later, however, we realize we've been duped. Our expectations collide with reality.

DIRTY LENSES

In his insightful book, *I Once Was Blind But Now I Squint*, Kent Crockett writes:

The world is filled with people who misinterpret what they see. . . . Perspective is in the eye of the beholder. Rejection, jealousy, and inferiority are just a few of the attitudes that create logjams in a viewer's eyes. We all perceive the world in our own unique way. . . . Why do people see things so differently? Very simple. It's the glasses we wear. But these are special glasses; they're not worn on our eyes. These glasses are worn on our heart. They're devilish lenses that distort the way we view life.[5]

We don't have to look very far to see the truth of Crockett's statement. People who are driven by greed see every person and situation as a target for profit. People who want to be appreciated as beautiful or talented see others as competition. Bitter people have thin skins and see every disagreement, no matter how mild, as a personal affront. Suspicious people see others as inherently untrustworthy, even if those people have proven themselves time after time. Paul made the same observation in a letter to his friend, Titus: "To the pure, all things are pure, but to those who are corrupted and do not believe, nothing is pure. In fact, both their minds and consciences are corrupted" (Titus 1:15).

The Bible contains many examples of people whose faulty perception dictated their actions. When Moses sent the spies to bring back a report of the Promised Land, two said, "We can take it!" but the other ten reported, "We seemed like grasshoppers in our own eyes" (Numbers 13:33). It's hard to fight if you see yourself as an insect and your opponents as giants! After David won the praise of people for killing the giant Goliath, King Saul had a "jealous eye" on the young man. The Pharisees saw Jesus as a threat to their power and authority. Luke

---

5   Kent Crockett, *I Once Was Blind But Now I Squint* (Chattanooga: AMG Publishers, 2004), pp. 4-5.

tells us, "The Pharisees and the teachers of the law were looking for a reason to accuse Jesus, so they watched him closely to see if he would heal on the Sabbath" (Luke 6:7). He did, and they became furious, eventually plotting to kill Him.

Jesus taught that accurate perception is crucial. In His most famous sermon, He explained, "The eye is the lamp of the body. If your eyes are healthy, your whole body will be full of light. But if your eyes are unhealthy, your whole body will be full of darkness. If then the light within you is darkness, how great is that darkness!" (Matthew 6:22-23)

CARICATURES

When we see someone who has a disproportionate response to a difficult person or a painful circumstance, we can be sure that person is a member of The Wounded Hearts Club. Hurt people are defensive. They see trouble where none exists, and when there's a genuine problem, they see it as catastrophic. Do you know any people like that? Do you see one when you look in the mirror?

Perhaps you have watched a caricature artist at a state fair or on the streets of New Orleans. He will look for a prominent feature—a big nose, wild hair, or a pointed chin—and exaggerate it even more. The effect is often very comical. But it's not amusing when we create caricatures of people in our minds. When we are hurt, we turn people into two-dimensional cartoons instead of seeing them

When we see someone who has a disproportionate response to a difficult person or a painful circumstance, we can be sure that person is a member of The Wounded Hearts Club.

as three-dimensional, real people. We exaggerate a flaw and dismiss the person with single-word labels: "He's a liar." "She's stupid." "He's a bum."

Wounded people also have a single word to describe themselves: *victim*. Their misperceptions poison hearts and ruin relationships. Only the grace of God can shatter the hardness of a bitter heart and heal the deep wounds of a broken one. When we have experienced grace, we can learn to extend it to those who have hurt us.

Professor Miroslav Volf suffered in the Balkan Wars, and he saw many people who refused to consider the need for different perception. He describes the horror of wrong perceptions and the need for God to give us new eyes:

> Forgiveness flounders because I exclude the enemy from the community of humans even as I exclude myself from the community of sinners. But no one can be in the presence of the God of the crucified Messiah for long without overcoming this double exclusion—without transposing the enemy from the sphere of the monstrous . . . into the sphere of shared humanity and herself from the sphere of proud innocence into the sphere of common sinfulness. When one knows [as the cross demonstrates] that the torturer will not eternally triumph over the victim, one is free to rediscover that person's humanity and imitate God's love for him. And when one knows [as the cross demonstrates] that God's love is greater than all sin, one is free to see oneself in the light of God's justice and so rediscover one's own sinfulness.[6]

---

6   Miroslav Volf, *Exclusion and Embrace* (Nashville: Abingdon Press, 1996), p. 124.

Marriages, friendships, and relationships of every kind are distorted by faulty perceptions. When wounded hearts cloud our vision, we don't see the good in others, we amplify anything negative, and we delight in exposing it. Women who have been abused by a boyfriend or husband see every man as a threat. Employees who have been mistreated by a boss believe they can't trust any employer. People who feel betrayed by a friend aren't willing to risk being vulnerable again.

I know. I've been there.

Several years ago, Kim and I moved out West and planted a church. Over time, the seeds began to grow, and a lot of people found Christ. It should have been a wonderful time in our lives, but it was horrendous. Conflict with a few people caused my anxiety levels to go through the roof, and heartache quickly spread. Factions erupted: Some supported me and others were against me. People flung accusations like quarterbacks throw footballs, and I was the target of most of them. I was devastated. I had done my best to honor those people, love them, point them to Christ, nurture them in their faith, and give them fulfilling roles. At every point, I had shown my appreciation for all they were doing to build God's kingdom. Now it was all crumbling down around me. I tried to resolve the misunderstandings, and in return I was accused of being defensive and controlling. It was a no-win situation.

I struggled for months. I relived countless conversations, trying to recall what I had said that caused such intense emotional outbursts. I second-guessed myself, wondering if God had really called me. After all, this wasn't exactly what unity and maturity in the body of Christ should look like! Kim and I anguished and prayed, but nothing changed.

Then God gave me a fresh insight: Those people were responding so strongly because they were deeply hurt. If you try to pet a dog that has been beaten by a cruel owner, the animal may growl and bite your outstretched hand. As I thought about the people who led the attacks against me, I realized they had endured a lot of heartache in recent years. They perceived God as harsh and unfair, and they transferred those perceptions to another authority figure: me.

The insight was helpful, but the damage had been done. For the next several years, I was like the abused dog. I refused to trust people, and I assumed any hand reaching toward me was a threat. I had come to believe that everybody was out to get me, that nobody had my best interests in mind, and that every person I met would purposely distort my words and actions so they could criticize me. Even people with pure motives and good hearts showed up on my list of suspects. If someone gave generously to the church, I wondered if he was using his gift for leverage. If a person had an idea for a project, I took offense because I assumed he was being critical of me. I was a walking poster child for paranoia, and it ate me alive. Of course, I blamed God for my heartache. I felt He had abandoned me. At one point, I prayed, "God, why did you bring me out West to humiliate me? Why didn't you just kill me?" I was ready to walk away from ministry, and I was ready to walk away from God—and I was the pastor!

CARDIAC ARREST

If our perspective becomes distorted, it's like having a cholesterol level of 300—we're on track for a heart attack! Throughout the Scriptures, the writers talk about the central importance of the heart. The word is found more than 1000 times. It describes the non-material aspect of human life. Most often, "the heart" involves the ability to reflect and choose, as well as our emotions, desires, hopes, and dreams. Scripture uses the word to strip away pretense and identify the source of conscious and decisive spiritual activity. Look at a few ways the Bible refers to the function of the human heart. (These examples are from the King James Version.)

- The heart thinks (Esther 6:6);

- The heart understands (Job 38:36);

- The heart imagines (Jeremiah 9:14);

- The heart remembers (Deuteronomy 4:9);

- The heart stores wisdom (Proverbs 2:10); and,

- The heart speaks to itself (Deuteronomy 7:17).

The heart is the place of our deepest reflection, and its considerations are often hidden, even from ourselves. God's Word, though, pierces into those depths to expose our secrets. The writer to the Hebrews tells us, "For the word of God is alive and active. Sharper **Most of us are naïve about the true condition of the human heart.** than any double-edged sword, it penetrates even to dividing soul and spirit, joints and marrow; it judges the thoughts and attitudes of the heart. Nothing in all creation is hidden from God's sight. Everything is uncovered and laid bare before the eyes of him to whom we must give account" (Hebrews 4:12-13).

Most of us are naïve about the true condition of the human heart. We often say, "Go with your heart," "Let your heart guide you," or "You can trust your heart." But Jeremiah had a different perspective. Through the prophet, God told the people of Israel:

"The heart is hopelessly dark and deceitful,
 a puzzle that no one can figure out.
But I, God, search the heart
 and examine the mind.
I get to the heart of the human.
 I get to the root of things.
I treat them as they really are,
 not as they pretend to be" (Jeremiah 17:9-10, *The Message*).

Was Jeremiah overly pessimistic? Haven't we evolved past that point so we can feel better about our hearts? Sorry. Our hearts are just as deceitful as ever.

Certainly, God has worked the miracle of grace in believers. He has given us new hearts, of flesh and not of stone (Ezekiel 36:26). However, we aren't yet free of our old nature. It's still there, and it's still active. Paul instructs us to make choices to live according to our new identity instead of letting our old natures rule over us. He compared the process to the habit of changing clothes. He said we need to "put off your old self, which is being corrupted by its deceitful desires; to be made new in the attitude of your minds; and to put on the new self, created to be like God in true righteousness and holiness" (Ephesians 4:22-24). Earlier in the same letter, Paul asked God to enlighten the eyes of our hearts (Ephesians 1:18) so we would know the hope of God's calling as His children, we would realize that God considers Himself to be rich because He has us, and we would experience the power of the Spirit. That's what it means to let God transform our hearts. It's a matter of seeing more clearly.

The enemy of our souls has had plenty of time to study the creatures called humans. He has become an expert. He knows the best way to steal, kill, and destroy (John 10:10) is to entice our hearts to turn from God to worthless things—but he convinces us such worthless things are the most valuable in the world. He tempted Eve in the Garden with the promise of autonomy, pleasure, and power. His temptations to us today are exactly the same. One of the most effective ways Satan tempts us is through the power of advertising. Virtually every moment of the day, we're bombarded with blatant or subliminal messages insisting we can't be whole or happy without a particular product or service. Advertisements are so pervasive we don't even notice them, but they have a powerful effect on our hearts. We believe them.

Jacques Ellul noted that advertising is designed to create an expectation—actually, a demand—for an ideal life of ease, plenty, and fun. This false perception robs us of spiritual values.[7] And in an article posted on CNN's web site, Monita Rajpal observed,

> Everywhere we go, everywhere we look, we are inundated with messages. We don't even have to think for ourselves. All we have to do is sit on our comfy couch and be told how to live our lives. From how to look, what to wear, what to eat, what our homes should look like, how to meet people, what to drive, practically every facet of our lives is taken care of. That is the power of advertising. . . . In this age of multiple mediums, advertising is everywhere—whether it's a pop-up campaign with people dancing at the train station (T-Mobile) that serves a multitude of platforms from television to the web, or a home-video-type commercial that is posted on You-Tube. We may not have to think for ourselves as much but we do have to be more discriminating to decipher what is

---

7   Jacques Ellul, *The Technological Society* (Alfred A. Knopf, Inc., 1964), cited at jan.ucc.nau.edu/~jsa3/hum355/readings/ellul.htm.

credible and what isn't. Bottom line though, advertising is a part of our existence. The good news is we're the ones with the power to choose.[8]

How do we know the impact of advertising on our hearts? I think its influence is far stronger than most of us imagine. We need to ask ourselves: If we cataloged our thoughts for a couple of days, what patterns would emerge? How much do we think about acquiring more status, winning more smiles, looking more attractive, and having the latest phone? And how much do we worry about not measuring up?

A popular praise song by Lynn DeShazo declares Jesus to be more precious than silver . . . more costly than diamonds . . . more beautiful than diamonds. The song summarizes the truth of the gospel by declaring that nothing we desire compares with Jesus Christ. Unfortunately, most of us usually pursue different treasures.

We can stop comparing ourselves to (and competing with) others in our communities, choosing instead to be salt (bringing out "God flavor") and light (bringing out "God color") for them. Through our lives people will be able to taste and see that God is good!

I'm not suggesting that we all sell our possessions, become hermits, and move to the boonies. Jesus spoke of the dichotomy of being *in* the world but not *of* the world (John 17:13-18). As long as our hearts remain riveted on Him, we can live, work, and play in this world

---

8   "The Power of Advertising," Monita Rajpal, CNN, cited on www.cnn.com/2010/WORLD/europe/09/22/power.of.advertising/index.html

without adopting worldly Madison-Avenue-inspired desires. We can stop comparing ourselves to (and competing with) others in our communities, choosing instead to be salt (bringing out "God flavor") and light (bringing out "God color") for them. Through our lives people will be able to taste and see that God is good!

King David faced numerous temptations throughout his life, and he eventually gave in to some big ones. But along the way, he learned the importance of putting God first in his life. In one of his psalms, he prayed:

> Teach me your way, Lord,
>> that I may rely on your faithfulness;
> give me an undivided heart,
>> that I may fear your name (Psalm 86:11).

The enemy wants to divide our hearts. Some of us go to church, read our Bibles, and then look at pornography. Others go to Bible study, serve at a homeless shelter, and go home and scream at the kids. Still others smile at the pastor while hiding thoughts of lust, jealousy, or bitterness. We will always wrestle with these temptations to some degree until we go on to meet Jesus, but we don't have to succumb and allow them to dominate our minds, our hearts, and our relationships.

When we measure acceptance by external markers like money, possessions, looks, and titles, we're seldom satisfied. Many people spend most of their day secretly (or not so secretly) measuring themselves against the people they walk past, comparing body shape, hair, teeth, cars, designer handbags, vacations, favorite restaurants, and any number of other factors. The people around them become competition instead of beloved friends and family. No matter how beautiful or handsome they are, and no matter how much stuff they acquire, it's never quite enough. When they get something they want, it feels great—for a few minutes or a few days. After that, the nagging feeling comes back, and they want a little bit more. Comparison may seem completely normal, but it's deadly!

Many "heart attacks" have an internal source, including lust, jealousy, inferiority, self-pity, resentment, discouragement, and worry. Others have an external origin. We may endure rejection, unjust criticism, or isolation from those we value. It hurts, and if we're not careful, the intense pain can drive us away from God. That's what happened to me when I suffered as a result of betrayal and rejection.

When the enemy's flaming arrows wound our hearts, we become self-absorbed. We stop looking out for others because we become pre-occupied with our own hurts. Our pain consumes us. In response, we may slink into the darkness to nurse our wounds or lash out at anyone who seems like a threat—or both.

When the enemy's flaming arrows wound our hearts, we become self-absorbed. We stop looking out for others because we become preoccupied with our own hurts.

"Devil" is more of a job description or title than a name. The word means, "to throw or penetrate." Paul tells us we need a shield of faith to "extinguish all the flaming arrows of the evil one" (Ephesians 6:16). Before Lucifer turned in rebellion against God, he was the brightest star among the angels. After he led a third of the angelic host against God, he didn't lose his brilliance and cunning. He uses those skills today to tempt, deceive, and accuse people so we'll give up on God. He and his minions are watching. They can't read our minds, but they certainly observe our actions and listen to our conversations.

They know the weak spots in our armor, and they fashion weapons to attack us where we're vulnerable.

And everybody is vulnerable. Personality profiles that show our temperaments and strengths also reveal where we're vulnerable to the enemy's attacks, if we look closely. For instance, those who manage to avoid the drive to win at all costs may also be thin-skinned and unable to accept criticism. Powerful people who shrug off criticism may be vulnerable to the temptation to use people instead of loving them. We are all works in progress. We all suffer from radical insecurity to some degree, so the enemy delights in putting people in our path who find fault with everything we do. Satan doesn't have to look very hard to find an opening to exploit. If his flaming arrow doesn't penetrate the first time, he will throw another and another until one penetrates the heart and wounds the person.

Satan's attacks cause a collision in us, but not in a good way. If we're not careful, we can let every hurt, every disappointment, every lust, and every misguided drive steal our hearts away from God. We need to pay attention to the condition of our hearts. We need regular checkups.

CHECK UP

We hear different voices in our minds. We hear the distant voice of our parents in our memories. We hear the current voices of spouse, kids, boss, and friends. We hear the shaky voice of our hopes and fears. We hear the deceptively enticing voice of the enemy. Too often, we listen to so many loud voices clamoring for our attention that we fail to notice the whisper of God's Spirit. But His voice is the most important of all.

David was a busy man, the ruler of the united kingdom of Israel, with incredible pressure from political and personal stress. In one of his most beautiful psalms, he reflects on the greatness of God. He describes the omniscience of God, His omnipresence, and His creative power. Because God had proven His greatness and grace, David invited God to have complete freedom in his heart. At the end of this powerful poem, he prayed:

> Search me, God, and know my heart;
> test me and know my anxious thoughts.
> See if there is any offensive way in me,
> and lead me in the way everlasting (Psalm 139:23-24).

How does God search our hearts and reveal what's there? We've already considered Hebrews 4:12-13, which says God's Word penetrates the deepest recesses of our hearts like a sword cuts into flesh and bone. When we think deeply about biblical truth, the Spirit exposes "the thoughts and attitudes of our hearts." It's not magic, but it's a mystery.

When I read, study, and dwell on God's Word, the voice of the Spirit becomes clearer and louder.

When I read, study, and dwell on God's Word, the voice of the Spirit becomes clearer and louder. He reveals my hidden motives so I can align my desires with His. He reminds me that I've said or done something stupid so I can make it right, and He gives me assurance that no matter what I've done, good or bad, His grace covers it all.

Where do we find wisdom to make hard decisions? The pages of the Bible don't give us every answer to every question, but they point us to God's character and the foundational principles of love, integrity, compassion, and justice. When we discover what God values, we can devote ourselves to those things. He's not impressed by our hard work or our knowledge; He cares far more about our hearts. The prophet Micah explained:

> But he's already made it plain how to live, what to do,
>> what God is looking for in men and women.
> It's quite simple: Do what is fair and just to your neighbor,
>> be compassionate and loyal in your love,
> And don't take yourself too seriously—
>> take God seriously (Micah 6:8, *The Message*).

When we read the Bible, we realize the struggle to overcome heart attacks isn't simple and easy. From the first couple in the Garden to the tribulation in Revelation, believers have had to fight, suffer, and strain to honor God. One of my biggest mistakes early in my commitment to follow Jesus was assuming He would make my life smooth, easy, and fulfilling—all day, every day. If problems arose, I was sure He would help me overcome them in a flash. But that's not the way life works. I learned the hard way. Every person of faith in the Bible faced tremendous struggles. Sometimes God miraculously rescued people *out of* their trials, but far more often, He rescued them *through* their trials.

A passage many of today's Christians don't want to read is just as true as it was two millennia ago. Paul wrote the Philippians, "For it has been granted to you on behalf of Christ not only to believe on him, but also to suffer for him, since you are going through the same struggle you saw I had, and now hear that I still have" (Philippians 1:29-30).

Yet God has given us powerful weapons to use in our struggles. In one of his letters to the Corinthians, Paul informed them, "For though we live in the world, we do not wage war as the world does. The weapons we fight with are not the weapons of the world. On the contrary, they have divine power to demolish strongholds. We demolish arguments and every pretension that sets itself up against the knowledge of God, and we take captive every thought to make it obedient to Christ" (2 Corinthians 10:3-5).

We need to realize that human resources are useless in fighting demonic attacks. We can't overcome the strongholds of lust, jealousy, resentment, depression, comparison, and all other human ills by gritting our teeth and trying harder. We need a different arsenal: the love, power, and grace of God.

Satan tells us God can't be trusted, that He's not powerful enough to care for us, and if He really loved us He wouldn't let us struggle at all. Those lies are "arguments" and "pretensions" that attack God's character and purposes. In response to this attack, we don't just sit back and hope it all works out. Soldiers pick up their rifles and charge the enemy! We pick up the truth of God's Word and fight every lie, every deception, every temptation, and every accusation Satan hurls at us. Sometimes we get wounded. We realize we've had impure motives, we've hurt the ones we love, and we've used people instead of loving them. But we heal our hurts, get up again, and get back in the fight. In this process, God does wonderful work to transform us. Through the battle, God

We can't overcome the strongholds of lust, jealousy, resentment, depression, comparison, and all other human ills by gritting our teeth and trying harder. We need a different arsenal: the love, power, and grace of God.

shows us that He is worthy of our love and loyalty—and nothing else comes close.

We learn more about God's character as we fight, and we also learn more about ourselves. We realize our connection with God is our most important asset. Peter reminds us, "But you are a chosen people, a royal priesthood, a holy nation, God's special possession, that you may declare the praises of him who called you out of darkness into his wonderful light" (1 Peter 2:9).

We aren't junk. We aren't scum. We aren't outcasts. We're God's chosen, adopted, beloved children, and He has given us the incredible privilege of representing Him to the world around us! When we look at the "armor" Paul lists at the end of the letter to the Ephesians, we may think of each part as an individual component. In fact, they comprise a complete package. We don't decide to put on one piece but not another. Together, the set of armor describes our new identity in Christ. We belong to Him, we're His children and His warriors, and He has given us all the protection and firepower we need to repel Satan's attacks. Victory lies not in our power, but in God's mighty strength. It's not our wisdom; it's His penetrating knowledge. It's not our compassion; it's His heart of love for us and others. We win the attacks on our hearts by grasping and living in our new identity in Christ.

A NEW BEGINNING

When I faced devastating rejection and criticism as a pastor in my late 20s, it was a collision that almost ended my career. The enemy hadn't just found a chink in my armor; the hole must have been big enough to drive a truck through! For a long time, I was thrown off balance. I questioned God, and I second-guessed everything I thought I'd known. I wanted to run and hide, but I had to keep moving toward people.

Sometimes the tension was so great that I thought I'd explode in rage, and sometimes I wanted to crawl into a hole and never come out. The battle for my heart was intense, and often, it looked like I was losing the fight. I was dying inside, and I was taking Kim and the kids down with me.

I went to counseling. I hoped the therapist could help me sort out all my emotions and the facts of the situation. For a while, I just vented. I couldn't understand what was going on, but I hoped the counselor could start to make sense of the outpouring of emotions and perceptions. Gradually, I started seeing connections between my past and the present, causes and effects, perceptions and reality. I discovered that my vantage point of life had been skewed. As I looked into the Scriptures, talked, and prayed, I began to see new patterns emerge. I was still in a fight, but now I had some hope that I might be on the winning side.

I began to discern the voice of the Spirit and distinguish His message from the cacophony of noise that had been screaming in my head. I saw that I'd been basing my security on people's opinions of me instead of my identity in Christ. And I realized I'd had very unrealistic expectations of a smooth, easy life of blessings after I had dedicated my life to the Lord. I was then able to fend off hurtful comments that I had let into my heart for so long, and I discovered a deeper, richer love of God than I had ever known.

When I was so deeply wounded, I withdrew from my most important relationships—with Kim, with our kids, and with my friends. As God led me out of my self-imposed isolation, I reconnected with them, and it was wonderful. I had been so afraid of being hurt again that I hadn't allowed myself to be vulnerable, but finally, little by little, I began to trust again. I thrive on relationships, and in my deep discouragement and distrust, the air hose of love and life had been stepped on. Pushing people away made me feel incredibly isolated and hopeless. The enemy knew my weakest point, and he blasted it unmercifully for a long time. Finally I began to heal, learn, and grow. I began to come back to life.

To be honest, I'm still more vulnerable to rejection and criticism than I would like to be, but I think that's just part of being human. God uses our weaknesses to humble us, to remind us to depend on Him, and to give us compassion for others who struggle. I'm no longer surprised when those painful feelings and perceptions surface, so I'm not caught off guard. Over the years, I've learned what to do when they come back: I listen to the Spirit, feast on God's Word about His character and my identity, fight against the lies, and hang out with honest, wise, loving people. I'm not immune to heart attacks, but now I identify them more quickly, and I have new skills and a growing track record of dealing with them.

Every heartache, every discouragement, and every bump in the road to our dreams is a collision between our desires and God's heart. We may not realize it, but each difficulty is a wakeup call. We instinctively ask hard questions. What really matters to us? What do we believe about God? What can we know about our purpose in life? Too often we try to pray ourselves out of a collision when it could be the very thing that propels us into a deeper understanding of God's heart.

God often reminds us to guard our hearts, but we

Every heartache, every discouragement, and every bump in the road to our dreams is a collision between our desires and God's heart.

may find it easier to "paint the well." Our hearts are like deep wells. If we find at the bottom the poison of wrong perceptions, lazy faith, and misplaced desires, we need to do the hard work of digging a new well to acquire fresh water. Instead, we too often settle for painting the pump so it looks nice. That's a stupid solution. Jesus used a similar metaphor when He told the jacked up, self-righteous, hateful Pharisees, "You think you have it all together, but you don't. You're like a tomb with stinking death inside, but you paint the outside white. That doesn't cut it" (Matthew 23:27-28, author's paraphrase).

But it's not just the Pharisees who paint their tombs and wells. We come to church and smile, even though we're dying inside. We tell people we're "just fine" while our most important relationships are disintegrating. We put on a show, wear masks, and try to impress people, but it's all a sham. I've been around long enough to realize that some of the world's greatest actors are in the church and should be nominated for an Oscar. At some point, we need to come clean. We should find someone who will listen, someone who doesn't offer simplistic solutions, and then open our hearts to share all the junk that's filling them. The only way to experience the cleansing of God's forgiveness is to be honest about our flaws and fears.

Every Thursday morning the people on our church staff spend an hour together in prayer. We call it "heart surgery." We ask God to reveal anything in us that isn't pleasing to Him, and we ask Him to assure us of His love, His power, and our identity in Him. God does amazing things. One person sometimes gets up to go apologize to someone else for an unkind comment or some other offense. Some return to their offices to make a phone call to get right with someone they've hurt. They don't wait for others to take the initiative; they go, whether they are the offended or the offender. By dealing with heart attacks regularly, persistently, and frequently, we don't let little wedges of hurt become mountains of distrust and resentment.

Heart surgery is beneficial for all of us. We need to live on God's operating table. We can say, "God, my heart is open to you. Have Your way in me. Speak truth into my heart—the hard truth about my sin, the comforting truth about Your grace, and the compelling truth about Your purpose for me. Use Your Word to cut deep into my thoughts and desires. Discern my hidden motives. Change my heart; then direct my hands. I'm Yours."

Heart surgery is beneficial for all of us. We need to live on God's operating table.

Is this your heart's cry?

THINK ABOUT IT...

1. What are some reasons most people assume their perceptions of life, God, people, and situations are entirely accurate and reasonable? What are some collisions that might cause them to question those assumptions?

2. Scripture says that our hearts are desperately wicked (Jeremiah 17:9). How should this observation affect how much we trust our hearts, contrasted with how much we need to depend on God's grace?

3. What are some examples of the enemy's attacks using temptation, deception, and accusation? Which of these have you experienced?

4. Look at 2 Corinthians 10:3-5. Describe the best strategy to take in the fight against Satan's attacks on our hearts.

5. Does the idea of regular "heart surgery" thrill you or terrify you? Explain your answer.

6. What are some benefits of being honest with God?

CHAPTER 3
MY FATHER'S HEART

My father gave me the greatest gift anyone
could give another person: He believed in me.

—Jim Valvano

The images of fathers in the media today are a long way from those
we saw on *Father Knows Best*. On television you'll see dads who are
bumbling, inept, and laughable. We seldom see fathers as heroes. Far
more often, they're fools.

In an article titled "The 10 Stupidest TV Dads," Paul Goebel lists Homer
Simpson as Number 10. (The list goes downhill from there.) In every
episode of *The Simpsons*, Homer is a hapless, clueless, selfish oaf. His
wife Marge puts up with him, his children dismiss him, and his boss
at the nuclear power plant expects him to blow up the world at any
minute. Another animated character, Peter Griffin, is the dad on *Family
Guy*. The writers and producers of the show seem to take great delight
in Peter's particular blend of evil and foolishness. His kids hate him, and
it's no wonder.

On *Modern Family*, Phil Dunphy desperately wants to be cool and relate
to his kids, but his lame attempts to act like a teenager make him look

like a fool. When his children's friends come over, he puts on skinny jeans and tries to speak in their vernacular. To say the least, they aren't impressed. In one episode, Phil assured his daughter he's cool because he uses acronyms when he texts—just like she does. He explained that he uses "WTF" all the time. When she looked shocked, he told her it means, "Why the frown?"

Number 1 on the list is Tim Taylor in *Home Improvement*. I remember enjoying that show back in the day. Goebel describes Tim's behavior: "Not only is Tim Taylor the stupidest dad on television but he revels in his stupidity. He seems to associate being dumb with being a man. So instead of educating himself, he decorates his body with manly accessories and puts his limbs in danger of being mangled. So the question is did his three boys grow up and decide to avoid being a living stereotype like their dad or did they meet an unfortunate end with the help of a miswired power mower?"[9]

These (and countless other) media images of fathers erode our respect for them. But while the glorification of inept fathers is often milked for laughs, the problem of fatherlessness is no laughing matter. The statistics are alarming. The latest census reports that 43 percent of children in the United States live without their father.[10] The gravity of that fact is magnified by other related statistics:

- 90 percent of homeless and runaway children are from fatherless homes.[11]

---

9   "The 10 Stupidest TV Dads," Paul Goebel, May 12, 2011, cited at perspectives.j2content.com/the-10-stupides-tv-dads/491

10   U.S. Census Bureau, 2010.

11   U.S. Department of Health and Human Services, Bureau of the Census.

- 71 percent of pregnant teenagers do not have a father at home.[12]

- 63 percent of youth suicides are children from fatherless homes.[13]

- 70 percent of juveniles in state-operated institutions have no father at home.[14]

Compared to children who live with married, biological, or adoptive parents, children who live in homes *without* a biological father are at least two to three times more likely to be poor, use drugs, become victims of child abuse, engage in criminal behavior, and/or experience educational, health, emotional, and behavioral problems.[15]

In our culture, many young people grow up feeling abandoned—emotionally, if not physically. **They wander aimlessly, looking for someone in authority to give them affirmation and guidance, but paradoxically, they resist receiving input because they don't trust authority.** The have broken hearts, but they try to hide their pain.

---

12   U.S. Department of Health and Human Services, Press Release, Friday, March 26, 1999.

13   U.S. Department of Health and Human Services, Bureau of the Census, 2010.

14   U.S. Department of Justice, Special Report, Sept. 1988.

15   "The Fatherless Generation," cited at thefatherlessgeneration. wordpress.com/statistics/

The absence of a loving, strong father leaves a deep gash in their souls. It's one of the most damaging collisions a person can experience. Our deep, God-given desire for a father's love and support crashes against reality.

That was not my experience at all. My father has regularly helped me navigate all the collisions I've faced. Without him, I don't know where I'd be today.

EXAMPLE AND ENCOURAGER

When I was growing up, my dad wasn't rich or particularly noteworthy in the world's eyes, but he is an incredible man. I have the ultimate respect for him. He consistently loved my mother and his six sons. His integrity was unquestioned, and his demeanor was always one of joy and hope—even in the toughest times. His love wasn't confined to his immediate family. Tim Dailey loves everyone on the planet! As I mentioned earlier in this book, he invited all kinds of people to come to our house—often not just for a meal, but to live with us until their fortunes changed and they got on their feet. I don't remember many quiet evenings in our home. People were always coming and going. They talked about the pain in their past, the problems of the present, and their hopes for the future. My mom and dad gave those people a second, third, and fourth chance to make it in life.

When Kim and I were dating, I often brought her to our home to hang out with our family. She was freaked out. She and her sister were raised in a sedate, protected home environment. She remembers, "I don't ever remember going to Ben's house and seeing only his family. Other people were always there. Ben's parents gave new meaning for having 'open doors.' They literally never locked their doors. Everyone was welcome at any time of the day or night."

My father invited addicts, alcoholics, divorced people, single moms, and others in need to stay with us for extended periods, but that was only part of the menagerie in our living room each day. When I came home from school or sports, I often found a bunch of my friends already there. They loved being with my parents because they felt totally loved and understood in our home. They could ask any questions without being condemned, and they could bask in the warmth of genuine, unconditional acceptance. My dad is a big guy—about 6 feet 5 inches tall, but not intimidating in any way. Several of my friends dropped by regularly just to get a hug from a big, strong, loving father. If they couldn't get one from their own dads, they knew they could get one from mine. A lot of kids came with no agenda at all. They just walked in the door and sat down to become part of our family for an hour or two.

A friend asked me if I ever felt that my father looked past me as he cared for all these people. It's a logical question, but the answer is, "Never." Even though our front door was revolving every day with people off the street who needed help and kids who just wanted time with my dad, I never felt neglected in the least. I was sure my mom and the boys were his top priority. He made that very clear. We always had his ear; we were always first in his heart—after Jesus, of course. Dad involved us in caring for those who needed help. We all played a role in helping them, and we shared my dad's joy in being God's hands, feet, and voice to bring hope to hopeless people.

In the years since I grew up in that home, my dad hasn't changed at all. Today, my parents are missionaries in the Middle East, and while pastoring a great church, they still open their home to anyone who needs some love and attention. They welcome the hurting and broken into their home. My parents care for them, support them, pray for them, and give them whatever they need, just like they did when I was a boy. Nothing has changed.

LOVE AND LIMITS

All my life, my father has been amazingly affirming and attentive to me. He often told me he loved me, but even more, he showed it by his actions all day, every day. But Dad had some clear rules for his boys. As long as we lived under his roof, he insisted that we attend church and be involved in helping people. He didn't use manipulation or any other means to compel us to comply. We were his partners, but he was dad, boss, and king. For the most part, we were glad to be part of what he was doing.

In fact, my dad broke some rules of religion. We liked that. The fellowship of churches was very strict, but Dad sometimes took us to movies. As adolescents, we really appreciated his freedom and flexibility. He was fun to be around, and in that way he was very different from a lot of pastors. Many of my friends whose dads were pastors had very different stories. They felt pushed, pulled, condemned, and manipulated to obey strict rules. There was no joy in their obedience, not in the least. Many of those young people grew up hating the church, despising their fathers, and alienated from God. In stark contrast, my brothers and I all love and serve God, and we love our dad.

Some parents lay down the law and demand, "Don't smoke," or "Don't drink." In fact, they may have dozens of ironclad proscriptions for their kids. My father had a different way of communicating his expectations. He understood the human heart. He knew that temptation is seldom conquered with rules alone. For instance, he told us, "I don't want you to smoke, but if you do, don't sneak around. Come to me. Let's talk about it, and if you want to smoke, you can light up here at home. Whatever you want to do, I want to be with you."

One Wednesday morning when I was about 13, I announced, "Dad, today I want to smoke."

He answered calmly, "Okay, son. We can work that out."

That night he came home with a cigar. He handed it to me and said, "Here you go, Ben. It's yours. Take it out on the porch and light up. I'll come out to sit with you." Then he turned to my five younger brothers and told them, "Hey boys, come out to the porch. Ben's going to smoke a cigar, and I'm sure you'd like to watch."

We all filed out to the porch. My dad struck a match and held it in front of my cigar. I took some long drags on it and blew out clouds of thick smoke. I was living large! I felt like a real cigar connoisseur. I kicked my feet up and went for it! My little brothers were horrified. One of them prayed fervently, "Jesus, forgive Ben. Help him quit smoking!" But I took a deeper drag and attempted to blow rings of smoke. I'd seen cool people do that in the movies, and I wanted to be just as cool.

Dad's first rule for smoking and drinking was that we had to do it with him, and his second rule was that we had to finish what we started. That proved to be a problem. The first puffs on the cigar made me feel like a king, but about halfway through, I started turning green! My father and brothers got some kind of sinister delight watching me get so sick. My stomach was churning, and my head was spinning. I said,

"Dad, I think that's enough."

He shook his head, "Sorry, Ben. You know how this goes. We'll sit here until you finish." I hoped to distract them and throw the cigar in the bushes, but Dad and my brothers kept a close eye on me.

By the time I took the last drag on the cigar, I was nauseated and ready to go to bed. I staggered into the house, but Dad announced, "Okay everybody, it's time to go to Wednesday night service!"

I moaned, "Dad, I can't go. I'm so sick."

He cheerfully explained, "Son, you know the rules. We always go to church on Wednesday night. Tonight is no exception. Get ready. We're leaving in a few minutes."

I ran to the bathroom, dry heaving. I finally made my way to the car and went to church with my family. (My dad did have some compassion and allowed me to lie on his office floor until I felt well enough to go to the youth service, where I promptly bragged to my friends that I had just effortlessly smoked a big ol' stogie.) I've never forgotten that day. My dad gave me the freedom to make my own choices, but he made sure I experienced the consequences. Through it all, I felt his love.

My dad's life was a 3-D movie of God's grace and compelling purpose—for his life and ours. We never wrestled with any thought of Dad being a hypocrite; he lived his values every day. He didn't just talk about love, mercy, and justice. He poured them into every person in our community. When I had opportunities to drift away from God and be involved in all kinds of sin, the primary motivation to stay on the narrow path was my respect for my dad.

When my parents moved away so he could be the pastor of another church, I stayed behind to finish my senior year. I was the student body president, played on the football team, and had plenty of friends. I stayed in the home of a family friend all week and drove to my parents' house every weekend. During that year, I was a 17-year-old young man, unsupervised and free as a bird. Meanwhile, some of my friends were doing drugs, smoking weed, having sex, stealing, vandalizing, and doing all the other things crazy teenagers do, but I always said "No." It wasn't that my adolescent hormones were inoperative. They were in full force. And it wasn't that I was a more noble person than my friends. I wasn't. (Believe me, I wasn't perfect.) As every temptation surfaced, I turned away for one reason: I didn't want to do anything to hurt my father in any way. He deserved nothing less from me. No matter how much I wanted to stray, my compelling motivation was to avoid dishonoring my father. I knew that if I gave in, it would break my dad's heart. I loved him and respected him too much to let that happen.

No matter how much I wanted to stray, my compelling motivation was to avoid dishonoring my father. I knew that if I gave in, it would break my dad's heart. I loved him and respected him too much to let that happen.

Throughout my life, my father's powerful, positive influence has been rigorously consistent. He always has a bigger picture of my life that focuses on God's purpose. He writes very encouraging letters, and every Christmas he sends each of his sons a personal note full of love and hope for our future. He always signs them, "Your #1 Fan, Dad." A few years ago, he wrote:

Benjamin ("Son of my right hand"), how can I tell you how proud of you I am? You have made me so happy. Your love and commitment to Jesus; your obedience to the call of God upon your life; your example to your younger brothers; your choice of a beautiful, committed, godly wife; your part in blessing us with our first grandchild (and a girl to boot); your powerful, anointed preaching; your love for and your resolve to stand upon the unchanging foundations of our faith; and your faithful and loyal service as a pastor have blessed me.

Thank you, Lord, for giving me Ben!

To all six sons, he concluded:

Your Mother and I pray every day for you and for God's protection, blessing, and care. Keep your heart always fixed on Him and the fulfillment of His destiny for you. Remember, each of you are loved, wanted, and uniquely gifted. You are not an accident or a mistake—you are part of an eternal plan. Each of you is your own man and will be used distinctly by God. I don't expect or desire that you be like anyone but Jesus. Thank you again for being such a special blessing to my life and to your mother.

Your #1 Fan,
Dad.

German writer Ruth E. Renkel observed, "Sometimes the poorest man leaves his children the richest inheritance." My life is rich today because my father gave me so much. His letters and verbal affirmation mean the world to me, but that's only part of the picture. Every day, I saw love, integrity, commitment, sacrifice, and consistency. Referring to his own dad, Clarence Budington Kelland noted, "He didn't tell me how to live; he lived, and let me watch him do it." I could say the same thing about my dad.

ROOTS AND WINGS

Every human being faces uncertainty. We experience colliding ideas, desires, dreams, habits, and visions of the future. The collisions can result from family conflicts or from any number of outside forces. Some are our own fault; others are completely out of our control. When my dad faced difficulties in his career, in family finances, or in strained relationships with people who didn't understand him, he never blamed others; he never shook his fist at God; and he didn't bail out. Watching him respond to the collisions in his life gave the rest of the family a sense of security and hope for the future. Dad gave us roots and wings.

Our family certainly experienced seasons of suffering and confusion, but my dad bridged the gaps of suspicion with trust. With him, everything was out in the open. We didn't hide our temptations, heartaches, and flaws. We were honest about them, so we could forgive and learn life's lessons. Many families never talk about things—especially "the elephant in the room" that threatens the stability of the family. But in our home, my parents held regular family meetings. (Honestly, I didn't always enjoy those "family meetings," and today my kids feel the same way about the family meetings I originate.) We talked about anything and everything. If there was tension in any relationship in our home, no one went to bed before it was resolved. Paul wrote the Ephesians,

Watching him respond to the collisions in his life gave the rest of the family a sense of security and hope for the future. Dad gave us roots and wings.

"Do not let the sun go down while you are still angry, and do not give the devil a foothold" (Ephesians 4:26-27). Our family internalized this principle and lived it.

THE GOSPEL ACCORDING TO DON CORLEONE

In our family, loyalty was, and is, gangster. Dad never let anything drive a wedge of anger or doubt between any of us. We always knew we could count on him, on Mom, and on each other. We learned that when you give your word, it's your bond. Today my favorite movies are *The Godfather Trilogy* because Dad was a Christian version of Don Corleone—if there is such a thing. He taught us to follow through with our commitments, no matter the cost.

After I had been a pastor for a few years, my parents and younger brothers came to visit. I thought of a great idea that was way out of the box for a preacher's family: I set up a casino in my living room. I got my hands on a roulette wheel and a blackjack table. When my parents opened the door and walked in, my mom was astonished—and not in a good way. She worried that her boys had flipped out and become gamblers. Dad was cool. He smiled and nodded, and he jumped right in. He didn't know much about gambling, but he was a quick learner. By the end of the night, the older brothers had cleaned out our younger siblings. By Vegas standards, the amount they owed me wasn't big, but it was huge to them. A couple of them assumed all this was just a gag, and that they didn't really owe the money. When we told them to pay up, they began complaining, "Don't take my money. It's not fair!" They looked to Dad for some help.

He asked them, "Did you gamble?" They nodded. He continued, "Did you have a chance of winning?" They nodded again. He then told them, "If you had the chance to win, you'd expect your brothers to pay.

You lost, so you need to pay up. No more questions, and no more complaints. Pony up, boys." They learned an important lesson that night. They haven't gambled since.

My life is rich because of my parents. My dad loves God's Word. Every night he led us in family devotions, and they weren't dull and routine. We saw his enthusiasm for learning and his tender heart in responding to God's truth. When the six boys were getting ready for school each morning, we could hear Mom and Dad praying for us. But the impact on the six of us was much more than a collection of individual principles. My parents live for Jesus. To them, following Christ isn't a dry, sterile discipline; it's life and joy, peace and comfort, meaning and purpose. They modeled it in tough times as well as good times.

My dad always lived what he preached on Sunday morning. There was no phoniness, no dichotomy between the public man and the private man. In today's culture, people talk about the value of "authenticity." That's what I saw in my father before the term was cool.

If I had any reason for complaint, it might be that my father's spiritual courage appeared to come so effortlessly. He certainly wasn't oblivious to the pain inflicted on him by denominational leaders, but he steadfastly refused to hate. If I got angry with someone who was unfairly criticizing him, he held his hand out to motion "Stop," and he said, "None of that. We don't know what's in the hearts of those people. Let's not judge them. God wants us to love people, even those who are our enemies."

So years later, when I experienced fierce ridicule and rejection of my own, I expected to deal with it as effortlessly as my dad seemed to handle it. I couldn't. My natural instinct was to cuss at my critics rather than pray for them. It was much harder for me to learn to love those who opposed me. During that time, I realized more than ever the depth of my father's character.

One of my greatest aspirations is to follow my dad's example in parenting. I never want my work or my career to become more important than Kim, Kyla, and Kade. I'm committed to protect them, to model a life of vibrant faith to them, and be completely open about everything that happens in our family.

GOOD DAD, BAD DAD, NO DAD

If you've had a great relationship with your dad, tell him. Write him a letter or give him a call to let him know how much you admire him and love him. Go beyond generalities. Tell him specific things he's done that have shaped your life, providing roots of security and wings of hope for the future.

If your relationship with your father is one of the biggest collisions of your life, be honest about the wound in your soul, take steps to forgive your dad, trust God to mend the hole in your heart, and hang out with spiritually mature people who can become new role models for you. This wound tends to be deeper and to cause more trouble than most of us can imagine. Some of us become driven to prove ourselves, and we use people to get ahead in the world instead of loving them. Some of us are so hungry for affection and affirmation that we do and say virtually anything to win approval. Others try to numb the pain with substances or fill the emptiness with addictive behaviors. Still others have given up on life, withdrawing to a world of isolation and emptiness.

Of course, most people who are deeply affected by a "father wound" exhibit a combination of these traits. When we feel abused or abandoned by a father, we naturally react in self-defensive defiance: "I'm not going to let anybody hurt me again!" But anger and demands that result from a father wound never produce healthy relationships in other areas of life.

Author and pastor Frederick Buechner describes the consequences of defiant self-protection:

> To do for yourself the best that you have it in you to do—to grit your teeth and clench your fists in order to survive the world at its harshest and worst—is, by that very act, to be unable to let something be done for you and in you that is more wonderful still. The trouble with steeling yourself against the harshness of reality is that the same steel that secures your life against being destroyed secures your life also against being opened up and transformed.[16]

I believe another group of people need to face the collision: dads. Many fathers today realize how deeply they've wounded their kids, but they've given up trying to restore the relationship. If this is true of you, be assured that it's never too late. No matter what you've done, no matter how badly you've failed, God hasn't given up on you. He loves you dearly and has forgiven you completely. Come back to Him, and then, with a fresh perspective, reach out to your kids.

---

16   Frederick Buechner, *The Sacred Journey* (New York: HarperOne, 1991), p. 46.

In the last verse in the Old Testament, the prophet Malachi utters a prophecy: "See, I will send you the prophet Elijah before that great and dreadful day of the Lord comes. He will turn the hearts of the fathers to their children, and the hearts of the children to their fathers" (Malachi 4:5-6).

Isn't that what we need today? Countless people are desperate for their fathers to come through for them, and countless dads long for their children to forgive them and offer an olive branch to rebuild the relationships.

A lot of people today are functional orphans. When I meet with them and see their pain, it breaks my heart. I wish I could take them to my parents' house and let them live there for a few weeks to soak up the love and peace. But God has provided other stable, nurturing environments where father wounds can be healed. Friendships, counseling sessions, and small groups can be healing communities.

One of the biggest needs today is for people to have a healthy, accurate view of their heavenly Father. I had a great model in my dad, but others aren't so fortunate. We can't go back and relive a painful past, but we can unhook from the pain by choosing to forgive. Then we can grieve the deep, gnawing losses and establish a new bond of strong, loving relationships in the church. It's not easy, and it's not quick. But God can do wonders if we unclench our fists in order to receive His healing love.

THINK ABOUT IT...

1. What are some portrayals of dads you've seen in modern media, especially on television?

2. To some degree, all of us have some kind of "father wound" because our dads are thoroughly human. How would you describe your wound? What have you done to forgive your father, grieve the losses, and restore your soul?

3. How can dads give their children "roots"? How can they give them "wings"? How well did your father give you roots and wings? Explain your answer.

4.   How has your dad modeled aspects of the character of God?

5.   What are some ways your life is richer because of your dad? Have you told him recently?

6.   Overall, has your dad helped you deal with life's collisions? Or has he been one of your biggest ones? Explain your answer.

CHAPTER 4
DEALING WITH JERKS

If you're going to be two-faced, at least make
one of them pretty.
—Marilyn Monroe

Each of us has plenty of opportunities to butt heads with others. Difficult people come in all shapes, sizes, ages, and colors. We don't have to look very far to find them. Actually, they seem to find us! Some of the biggest collisions in my life have occurred when my hopes and dreams have collided with the expectations and demands of such people. We butt heads because we have different perceptions of reality. Two hearts can look at life and draw very different conclusions.

HOPE AND VENOM

After pastoring in the western part of the country for seven years, my spiritual father (whom I'll tell you more about later in this book) asked Kim and me to come back to Texas to pastor with him. We asked God for direction for our ministry when we arrived, and He gave us a vision for reaching the community.

Over and over again as I read the Gospels, I saw Jesus leaving the ninety-nine to go after the one lost sheep. He didn't sit in a comfortable recliner in the temple. He went out to touch lepers, blind people, prostitutes, tax gatherers, and every other outcast in His society. He also extended His love to the religious elite, but they often responded with withering condemnation. In fact, they plotted to murder Him.

When I came back to Texas and looked at the demographics of our church, it was about ninety-eight percent Caucasian. The community around our church, though, was a kaleidoscope of different colors. An article in *D Magazine* reported that Irving is the most diverse city in Texas, but our church didn't reflect diversity at all. I sensed God wanted us to create a faith community that welcomed all kinds of people. They needed a place where artificial barriers of exclusion are torn down, where they could feel loved even if they didn't look like, talk like, or believe like anyone else.

Jesus broke down walls that separate people. The disenfranchised loved to hang out with Jesus because they sensed His genuine acceptance. In many churches, people have to jump through hoops before they can belong. They have to conform established church beliefs, dress, and language before other people accept them. At Calvary, I was intent on building an environment so positive, so accepting, that people could belong *before* they believed. When people feel warmly welcomed—no matter what they believe—they're much more open to hear the truth of the gospel. Love breaks down all kinds of barriers.

I wanted to create a culture of belonging for people who feel like outcasts and misfits. As we scratched just below the surface of people's lives, we uncovered deep hurts from divorce, disease, depression, debt, and other distresses. I was happy for the socially and spiritually comfortable people to attend, but they weren't my main focus. Many young people drop out of church because they don't see how God or the church is relevant to their lives. They're the Facebook and Twitter generation. They simply don't relate to suits, organ music, strange pronouns in the Bible, and messages they can't understand. As I prayed, I was sure God wanted us to be like Jesus and care for people who were outside the reach of the churches in our area. That's Jesus' heart, and it became my heart.

As I prayed, I was sure God wanted us to be like Jesus and care for people who were outside the reach of the churches in our area. That's Jesus' heart, and it became my heart.

I was so excited! The new direction felt so right. I couldn't wait to talk to Kim every day to share additional ideas of how we might reach out to more people. If we did what the Lord wanted us to do, thousands of people in our community would experience the grace of Jesus and be transformed. Who could argue with that?

Yet when I announced my plans to our church, some of the people responded like I'd invited Satan to rule over us. Immediately, the kickback hit me in the face. Members questioned my relationship with God, my leadership, and my motives. Kim was working in the church office at the time. She got a number of phone calls from people who didn't realize she was my wife. They told her: "That Ben Dailey deceived us. He has no business coming in here and changing our church"; "He's of the devil, I tell you!"; "I bet he hasn't even prayed about all these new plans. It's all a big show anyway. He only wants to build his reputation"; "What's he trying to do, kick the Holy Spirit out of our church?" One individual took our family Christmas card, tore my family's picture into pieces, put them in an envelope, and sent them to my office. That's what they thought of me, our family, and God's leading in our lives.

I received anonymous letters saying, "If you let any more black people into our church, we'll rise up against you and split this church wide open!" One person at least had the integrity to call and talk to me in person. He told me, "If you invite any more people of color (he meant Hispanics and African Americans) to Calvary, my friends and I will make life hell for you!"

In a leadership meeting, a man glared at me and snarled, "I don't care about lost people coming to this church. I want my parking space!" Other leaders in the church cornered me and cussed me out like I was a dog. One of them told me, "You keep saying we're going to cast a wide net to catch the fish God wants us to reach. I tell you, pastor, we don't need any more *%#@ fish! You've already caught enough. Start taking care of what you have."

Some members used the most offensive language to describe the people who were finding their way to our church, defaming them with derogatory, racial slurs. A caller told Kim, "I don't mind my kids going to school with black people, but I don't want them going to church with (fill in the blank)." This wasn't language used by a lynch mob in Alabama in the 30s; it was my city just a few years ago. Virtually all of the vicious comments came from people over 50, but some came from young people—primarily the children of the most negative older adults. Bigotry doesn't fall far from the tree.

At first I was stunned, and then I felt crushed. I had no idea the clear teaching of Scripture and a heart to reach out would elicit such a venomous reaction. I was shaken to the core. I wondered if I'd heard God correctly, and I questioned if He had called me to be a pastor at all. Surely this wasn't what He wanted at our church. I told Kim, "If this is what it means to be a pastor in this city, I don't want any part of it."

At first I was stunned, and then I felt crushed. I had no idea the clear teaching of Scripture and a heart to reach out would elicit such a venomous reaction.

Before I announced the new strategy, I had expected *some* pushback from a few of our key leaders and staff, and I was prepared to fight that battle. I was sick of the *narcissistic entitlement* I saw surfacing. The term refers to the attitude of people who contribute little to an organization, but who are convinced the organization owes them a great deal just for being graced by their presence. I expected to have a few hard conversations about unrealistic expectations, but I was totally unprepared for the vicious venom, rooted in racism, that spewed from the hearts of so many leaders and members in the church.

The Bible says that people who have given up on their hopes have "lost heart." That's what happened to me. My heart felt like a desert . . . a concrete block in my chest . . . a bottomless pit. No matter what metaphor I used, it wasn't adequate to describe the way I felt. But I wasn't the only one who was devastated by the attacks. When people are too cowardly to speak up to their pastor, they often feel they can approach his wife, so Kim took many blows and endured a number of vicious rants meant for me. The dissenters hoped their angry words would motivate her to twist my arm and change the church's direction. Kim didn't want to expose me to more insults, so she internalized every bitter, poisonous word. For the first fourteen months of our time back in Texas, she silently battled a horrific satanic attack. I watched her sink into a hopeless, dark depression. Not knowing who was for us or against us, it became a lonely, confusing season for Kim. I felt helpless. I watched my once vibrant wife dying emotionally, but I didn't know how to fix her. Pastors' wives are often the unintended victims of attacks on their husbands. They silently watch people destroy their husbands, and it devastates them.

IN YOUR LIFE

You may not be able to relate to my experience of dealing with jerks in the church, but you may find difficult people at home, at work, in your extended family, or in an organization where you belong. For many of us, the most difficult relationship in life is with the person who sleeps next to us. Years of misunderstanding and unresolved conflicts can fester into open warfare or settle into defensive distance.

At work, we feel overlooked and unappreciated. Someone else, someone not as qualified, got the promotion we hoped for. The boss lavished praise on the other guy. We've given our heart and weekends to the company, but we feel used and abandoned.

Fights with parents or children hurt us deeply. We hoped for *Ozzie and Harriet*, but we got Ozzy Osbourne. Disagreements between adult siblings can trigger fierce reactions, especially from the spouses, and people spend their energy protecting their turf and hurling verbal hand grenades instead of seeking common ground.

When we suffer such disappointments, we become so beleaguered that we forget who our allies are. In our church and on our staff team, I became suspicious of everyone. I didn't know who was still a friend and who had been swayed by the opposition—and it could change from day to day, or even from one hour to the next. I was defensive with people in our office, and I even became short and angry with Kim. That was the last thing she needed or deserved!

In conflict, people respond in two very different ways. In his book, *Tired of Trying to Measure Up*, Jeff VanVonderen makes a most insightful observation:

> I've noticed that when people experience something that is shaming, they respond in one of two directions. They either get *big* (that is, they become raging, loud, start trying twice as hard, want to debate, or try to win). Or else they get *small* (that is, they withdraw by getting quiet, by leaving, look away or down, quit what they're doing, start to cry, become people-pleasing).[17]

I'm sure you have you seen people react in these two ways. When those in our church attacked me, some of them got big. They fumed and blustered, accused and threatened. But there were hundreds of other people who got small. As the conflict raged around them, they wilted and withdrew. They felt just as threatened as the first group, but their feelings weren't as obvious, so Kim and I didn't notice them as much. Actually, the reaction of the "big" people created more insecurity for the "small" people than the proposed change in direction for the church.

The Bible includes many examples of people who got big or small in times of crisis. Elijah got really big when he confronted the prophets of Baal on Mount Carmel and called down fire from heaven, but then he got very small when he became depressed and hid in a cave. The

17   Jeff VanVonderen, *Tired of Trying to Measure Up* (Minneapolis: Bethany House, 1990), p. 198.

Our goal should be to avoid getting big or getting small. Instead, we make a commitment to face conflict with a powerful blend of grace, truth, and confidence.

Pharisees got big when they falsely accused Jesus and dragged Him into court to condemn Him. The disciples got small and ran for their lives!

Our goal should be to avoid getting big or getting small. Instead, we make a commitment to face conflict with a powerful blend of grace, truth, and confidence.

TYPES OF DIFFICULT PEOPLE

A variety of studies identify "problem people" in our lives. I want to paint a picture of six of the most common types we face.

Blame throwers

Some people are looking for a fight. When disagreements arise, they're never wrong. They point fingers, accuse, and blame anyone and everyone but themselves. Nothing is ever their fault. If they run a red light and kill a blind person crossing the street, they snarl, "He should have seen me coming!" It's very difficult to have an honest conversation with blame throwers because they seldom take responsibility for any problem.

Blame sponges

These people feel very uncomfortable with conflict. To end any disagreement as soon as possible, they assume all the blame. No matter what happened, they quickly say, "It's all my fault. Now, let's talk about something else." It's hard to have a conversation with them, too, but for the opposite reason. They want to avoid meaningful discussion about tension, problems, or disagreements. Their quick admission of guilt may seem noble and humble, but it's really motivated by fear.

Einsteins

Do you know anyone who is never wrong? Such people often are genuinely bright, but they use their knowledge and quick thinking to wield power over others. They're never in doubt. In conflict, they speak authoritatively about the source of the problem—and it's always someone else. When trying to talk to an Einstein, we may feel outgunned. Be sure to appreciate the person's contributions, and use an indirect method of communication, such as, "I was wondering about this idea."

IEDs

In families, companies, and other organizations, some people look harmless but have a hidden, deadly impact on the people around them. Just as terrorists use Improvised Explosive Devices to destroy passing vehicles, people around us may use gossip, innuendo, and passive-aggressive behavior to sabotage our best intentions. To them, it's a game. They may not really care about the issue at hand; they just like to have power over people and control the situation.

Misties

When everything is going well, some people are active contributors. When the heat is on, however, they evaporate into thin air. Conflict seemingly causes them to lose their ability to think, to communicate, and to participate in the resolution. They mumble excuses. If they can leave, they get out. If they have to stay, they try to become invisible. Of course, when others attempt to engage them, they feel even more uncomfortable and redouble their attempts to hide.

Wet blankets

A few people have "No" faces. They find flaws in every idea and faults in every person—and they delight in pointing them out. Quite often, wet blankets aren't openly hostile. They sit quietly until someone asks for their opinion, and then they offer their scathing rebuttal to even the most carefully considered ideas. When hopelessness prevails, they feel validated and powerful.

Each of these groups of people requires us to be observant and tailor our response. One size doesn't fit all. In each case, the solution isn't to get big and demand compliance nor get small and hope the problem goes away. We need to wade in, but with wisdom to administer an effective blend of grace and truth. For instance, when people are resistant to ideas, instead of barking our displeasure, we can say, "I need your help in figuring out how to make this work." In response, the person may become an ally instead of an enemy.

THE HARD CHOICE TO FORGIVE

All of us are members of the Wounded Hearts Club. We are fallen people living in a fallen world, so hurts are inevitable. Jesus said, "In the world you will have trouble. But take heart! I have overcome the world" (John 16:33).

Some became bitter and cynical, and some ran away and hid. But others responded with courage, honesty, grace, and kindness.

When I felt rejected and condemned, I looked around at other people who went through similar experiences, and I noticed that not everybody reacted the same way. Some became bitter and cynical, and some ran away and hid. But others responded with courage, honesty, grace, and kindness. They learned and grew through the process of dealing with difficult people. It made me wonder, *What's the difference?* The people who thrive and grow have learned how to forgive.

When we encounter difficult people, we get hurt. Even in relationships with blame sponges, misties, and wet blankets, we feel distrusted and isolated. No matter how hard we try to engage, they push us away. Our natural reaction when hurt is to lash out in retaliation or run away. Jesus gave us a different way to respond. He said:

> "You're familiar with the old written law, 'Love your friend,' and its unwritten companion, 'Hate your enemy.' I'm challenging that. I'm telling you to love your enemies. Let them bring out the best in you, not the worst. When someone gives you a hard time, respond with the energies of prayer, for then you are working out of your true selves, your God-created selves. This is what God does. He gives his best—the sun to warm and the rain to nourish—to everyone, regardless: the good and bad, the nice and nasty. If all you do is love the lovable, do you expect a bonus? Anybody can do that. If you simply say hello to those who greet you, do you expect a medal? Any run-of-the-mill sinner does that" (Matthew 5:43-47, *The Message*).

God doesn't want us just to *tolerate* those who have become our enemies; He wants us to *celebrate* them. To do that, we need radical heart surgery. Something deep within us needs to change so we genuinely love the people who have caused our pain. That doesn't mean we let them abuse us. Letting people continue to sin certainly isn't a way to love them. We speak the truth to them, forgive them, and offer a way forward in the relationship. If they take our hand, we have a lot of rebuilding to do! Trust wasn't eroded in an instant, and it won't be rebuilt in a day. It takes time, consistency, and tenacity, but over time, restoration is possible—but only if both sides determine to move toward each other.

Let's back up and explore the requirements for us to truly forgive the wounds inflicted by difficult people. Paul wrote that the beginning point is a genuine experience of God's grace. We can only forgive others if we're convinced God has forgiven our sins (Ephesians 4:32). We can only accept them if we're thrilled that God has accepted us because of Christ (Romans 15:7). And we can only love people if the well in our hearts is overflowing with the incredible love of God (1 John 4:10-11). Without the experience of God's love, forgiveness, and acceptance, we simply won't have the capacity or motivation to extend grace to those who have hurt us.

Without the experience of God's love, forgiveness, and acceptance, we simply won't have the capacity or motivation to extend grace to those who have hurt us.

I've talked with a few people who said, "Pastor, I must not be able to forgive because I can't forget the things that happened. God forgets, so I should, too." This is a misunderstanding of the passage in Jeremiah. Through the prophet, the Lord promised, "For I will forgive their wickedness and will remember their sins no more" (Jeremiah 31:34). But God is omniscient. It's part of His essential character to know all things, so how can he "forget" anything? God doesn't have a lobotomy, and He doesn't undergo electric shock therapy. He knows the event happened, but when He thinks of us, He doesn't hold it against us any longer. He "forgets" only in the sense that He no longer holds the sin against us. The sin isn't forgotten, but judgment has been removed.

Similarly, when we forgive, we still remember the events took place, but gradually the sting goes away. After a while, we might even have a hard time recalling how the person wounded us. In that sense, we too have forgotten the offense so that it doesn't haunt us any longer.

I've heard well-intentioned Christian leaders tell people, "If you haven't forgotten, you haven't forgiven." That's not true. In fact, such an unrealistic (and unbiblical) picture of forgiveness is a straightjacket that keeps people in bondage to the wounds of the past. Genuine forgiveness can be an excruciating experience. We clarify the wrongdoing, acknowledge the pain and the damage it inflicted, and choose to absorb the debt. It may require a long time before the grieving process takes its course and thoughts of the offense no longer cloud our thinking.

When we make the courageous choice to forgive, we don't excuse the offense ("She couldn't help it"); we don't minimize the pain ("It didn't really hurt that bad"); and we don't deny the event ("Offense? What offense? I don't know what you're talking about"). We look at it "full in the face," call it what it is, and then draw from the deep well of God's grace to forgive the person.

Paul emphasized the importance of forgiveness: "Get rid of all bitterness, rage and anger, brawling and slander, along with every form of malice. Be kind and compassionate to one another, forgiving each other, just as in Christ God forgave you" (Ephesians 4:31-32). Our forgiveness of others is, as Miroslav Volf described, "an echo" of God's forgiveness for our sins.[18] When we extend forgiveness, the hearts of some people melt, but others remain as hard as stone. God doesn't make people trust in His grace, and we can't force people to respond with grateful hearts when we forgive them.

---

18   Miroslav Volf, *Free of Charge* (Grand Rapids: Zondervan, 1996), several citations.

If we refuse to forgive, resentment builds in our hearts. We say we want justice, but secretly we long for revenge. In our desire to pay people back, we concoct a poison we hope to make them drink. Too often, they don't care that they hurt us. They may not give the matter a second thought. But the poison still works its power . . . in *us*. Soon it stains every relationship, demeans every motive, and clouds every dream. That's what happened to me. Nightmares about hurts and daydreams about revenge poisoned my relationship with Kim, with our children, and with every person I knew. I had to find a way to let go.

If we refuse to forgive, resentment builds in our hearts. We say we want justice, but secretly we long for revenge.

Some of us are slow to forgive because we assume that forgiveness somehow diminishes the painful offense. Author and pastor Lewis Smedes wrote, "When we forgive evil we do not excuse it, we do not tolerate it, we do not smother it. We look the evil full in the face, call it what it is, let its horror shock and stun and enrage us, and only then do we forgive it."[19]

There are no guarantees. Even when we choose to forgive, the person who hurt us may not apologize or even acknowledge the offense. Still, we forgive unilaterally. We don't wait for the offender's warm-hearted, repentant response. When we forgive with no preconditions, it sets us free, it honors God, and it offers the only hope of restoration.

---

19 Lewis Smedes, *Forgive and Forget* (New York: Harper & Row, 1984), pp. 79-80.

I've talked with people who were reluctant to forgive·because bitterness made them feel strong, and they assumed forgiving the offender would make them weak. That's not true at all. When we forgive, we take a bold stand for God and for grace. We also show the person and everyone else who's watching, "You won't dominate my life any longer. Your actions will no longer dictate my identity. I'm going to follow Christ and choose to forgive so I can be free." When we forgive, we step out of the role of victim and become a victor. We can then offer a hand to those who hurt us.

Dr. Martin Luther King, Jr. understood how choosing to forgive sets people free. In a Christmas sermon, he told his congregation:

> I've seen too much hate to want to hate, myself, and every time I see it, I say to myself, hate is too great a burden to bear. Somehow we must be able to stand up against our most bitter opponents and say: "We shall match your capacity to inflict suffering by our capacity to endure suffering. We will meet your physical force with soul force. Do to us what you will and we will still love you. . . . But be assured that we'll wear you down by our capacity to suffer, and one day we will win our freedom. We will not only win freedom for ourselves; we will appeal to your heart and conscience that we will win you in the process, and our victory will be a double victory."[20]

Forgiveness necessarily involves grief because the wound creates a sense of loss.

---

20   Martin Luther King, Jr., "A Christmas Sermon for Peace," December 24, 1967.

Forgiving is one of the most difficult things we can do, but it is also when our hearts are most in tune with God. On the cross, Jesus died the death we deserved and gave us the love we didn't deserve to receive. When we forgive those who have hurt us, we absorb a kind of death, too. That's what it means to forgive "just as in Christ God forgave you" (Ephesians 4:32).

Forgiving is one of the most difficult things we can do, but it is also when our hearts are most in tune with God.

In *The Reason for God*, pastor Tim Keller explains the significance of forgiveness:

> Forgiveness means refusing to make them pay for what they did. However, to refrain from lashing out at someone when you want to do so with all your being is *agony*. It is a form of suffering. You not only suffer the original loss of happiness, reputation, and opportunity, but now you forgo the consolation of inflicting the same on them. You are absorbing the debt, taking the cost of it completely on yourself instead of taking it out of the other person. It hurts terribly. Many people would say it feels like a kind of death. Yes, but it is a death that leads to resurrection instead of the lifelong living death of bitterness and cynicism.[21]

The writer to the Hebrews warned, "See to it that no one misses the grace of God and that no bitter root grows up to cause trouble and defile many" (Hebrews 12:15). The Greek word for *offense* means

---

21   Tim Keller, *The Reason for God* (New York: Riverhead Books, 2008), p. 196.

"trap." Every wound we receive is a trap laid by Satan to catch us and poison us with bitterness.

Some of us wear offenses like Boy Scout merit badges. We claim, "You offend me," or "This church offends me," and we glory in our position as victims. When being a victim is central to someone's identity, he or she has no incentive to get rid of anger. Soon the tiny shoot of anger grows into a huge root of bitterness.

Paul said, "Don't let the sun go down on your anger" (Ephesians 4:26). Some of us have thrown away dozens of calendars since the offense happened! The unwillingness to forgive puts a lid on our hearts and blocks the flow of God's love. We begin to believe there are only two kinds of people in our lives: those who are out to get us, and those who owe us. We become rigid, resentful, and self-righteous. We feel superior to the ones who hurt us. We tell people, "I'd never treat anyone like that!" And we feel completely validated in harboring our bitterness.

Instead of forgiving, some of us go to great lengths to keep track of offenses. I know of an elderly lady who has kept a notebook all her adult life. She calls it her "poop list." Every time someone hurts her in any way, she writes down the event and the details. At church, she sometimes speaks to a friend or an acquaintance, then she turns and whispers to her son, "She's on my list." From time to time, she goes back to read the entries to refresh her memory and keep her bitterness strong. She has invested countless hours stirring the poison in her soul.

We may gasp or laugh at her, but the fact is that most of us are not so different. We keep a similar list of offenses—it's just a *mental* one. We chronicle others' crimes in our cerebral diary, and we can think back over and over again to refresh our memories. Wounds create debts. The offenders have taken something from us, and now they owe us.

Clinging to the desire for justice and judgment gives us an identity: "I'm the one who was wronged." Resentment creates a nonstop engine of power that drives us to seek vengeance.

Forgiveness, then, goes against every fiber of our natural being. If we wait until we feel like forgiving, it will never happen. Everything in us cries out for revenge, so forgiveness is a supreme act of the will. When we forgive, we relax our death grip on the person, and we stop craving revenge.

Forgiveness, then, goes against every fiber of our natural being. If we wait until we feel like forgiving, it will never happen.

Jesus didn't want to go to the cross. He prayed, "Father, let this cup pass from me." But He submitted, suffered, and died to pay for our sins. In a similar (though far less sacrificial) way, our forgiveness also involves choosing to suffer loss instead of taking revenge on those who have hurt us.

Some people protest, "It's not fair!" And they're right. It's not fair at all, but it's the path God wants us to walk. We can be assured, though, that justice will ultimately be served—not by us, but by God. Paul reminds us, "Do not repay anyone evil for evil. Be careful to do what is right in the eyes of everyone. . . . Do not take revenge, my dear friends, but leave room for God's wrath, for it is written: 'It is mine to avenge; I will repay,' says the Lord" (Romans 12:17, 19). Forgiveness takes the offender off our hook and puts him on God's. That's where he belongs.

I heard a story about a lady who was bitten by a stray dog. She went to the doctor to check on the bite, and she took the dog with her. The doctor examined the lady and the dog, and he told her: "I'm sorry, ma'am, but this dog has rabies." The woman reached into her purse, got out a piece of paper and a pen, and started writing furiously. The doctor assured her, "Not so fast. You don't have to write your will right now. There are treatments for rabies." The lady responded. "Oh, doctor, this isn't my will. I'm making a list of all the people I want to bite."

When we forgive, we surrender the right to bite people. No one said it's easy.

Forgiveness is substitutionary; it always involves a cost. Jesus died on the cross as our substitute to pay for our sins. As we learn to forgive like He does, we bear the cost of the wound inflicted on us. We grieve, we forgive, and we refuse to bite back.

Can we require restitution? Yes, but only after we've done the hard work of forgiving and grieving. If we demand repayment before we have forgiven, it is with a spirit of judgment rather than grace. Our focus is on filling up the hole in our hearts—and our wallets. But if we first forgive, our motive changes. We ask for restitution for the other person's sake: It's in his best interest to make things right, and it's a step in rebuilding trust.

What if forgiveness seems impossible, frustrated, or blocked? Perhaps the person who hurt you is dead . . . or is as good as dead because he or she won't talk to you. Don't despair. Again, God is our model. All day every day, He offers His forgiveness. Some people take advantage of such a wonderful gift, but others don't bother to even notice. Some are thrilled to receive it, but others angrily reject God's hand offered in love. As the saying goes, "All we can do is all we can do." Even if our human connections are blocked, we can have a clear conscience if we've chosen to forgive the ones who hurt us.

Painful memories and angry feelings almost always linger after we've taken the bold step to forgive. Satan tries to use those nagging emotions to convince us we haven't really forgiven at all. Resist him. Tell him and yourself that you've chosen to forgive. The slate is wiped clean. Thank God for His mercy and strength, and keep moving forward. When those feelings return an hour or a week later, don't get bummed out. Remind Satan and yourself that you've done the hard work of forgiving the person who wronged you. Pray for that person. Ask God to pour out His blessings on him or her. And trust God to bless you, too.

Painful memories and angry feelings almost always linger after we've taken the bold step to forgive.

God delights in His children forgiving those who hurt them. In fact, just after Paul tells the Ephesians to forgive, he makes an important connection: "Follow God's example, therefore, as dearly loved children and walk in the way of love, just as Christ loved us and gave himself up for us as a fragrant offering and sacrifice to God" (Ephesians 5:1-2). We follow His example most closely, and we act like His beloved children most clearly, when we forgive like He forgives.

I'll be honest. When I go to the coffee shop and see someone who left our church after viciously attacking me, I don't have warm, fuzzy feelings toward him. I attempt to make a conscious choice to say "Hello" and stick out my hand, but I sometimes feel more like keeping my hand in my pocket. I'm still a work in progress, but I'm taking steps every day to try to be more like Jesus.

Of course, we aren't always the victims of injustice who need to offer forgiveness. Many times we hurt others and commit offenses, so we need to *seek* forgiveness. First we go to God to thank Him for Christ's complete payment for our sins, and then we go to the person we have offended to ask for forgiveness. We go humbly; we don't say, "This is my part, but here's what you did to me." We speak only about our role in the problem, and we take full responsibility for it.

Should we wait until the other person confronts us? No, we are to take the initiative. Jesus told us, "Therefore, if you are offering your gift at the altar and there remember that your brother or sister has something against you, leave your gift there in front of the altar. First go and be reconciled to them; then come and offer your gift" (Matthew 5:23-24).

TRY THIS INSTEAD

If we let wounds fester very long in our hearts, our minds begin to construct an alternate reality. Our vision of life becomes distorted. We become suspicious of even our best friends and/or we trust untrustworthy people. We focus on what God *hasn't* done for us instead of all the grace and blessings He *has* showered on us. We think, act, and talk like victims—because that has become our dominant identity.

But there's a better way to deal with the pain caused from butting heads with difficult people. Let me share a few suggestions.

Be honest about your pain.

You won't be able to grieve, forgive, or learn any lessons if you don't start with honesty. Don't minimize the pain, excuse the person, or deny the event. Go to God and pour out your heart to Him. He understands, and He cares. You can count on Him when you face your deepest wounds—even those you've tried to hide for years. The longer we deny the pain, the more it poisons our lives. Some people love to tell everyone about how they've been hurt, but many others try to keep a lid on their pain. Sooner or later, we need to come clean and admit how much we have been affected by unpleasant events and hurtful people.

Find a friend or mentor.

When we face life's deepest wounds, we shouldn't try to tackle them alone. During my difficulty with all the condemnation at our church, Don George was a constant friend and mentor. His perspective is, "Like a fireman, you always run toward a fire, not away from it." He often told me, "Ben, there's the fire. Run toward it." He wouldn't let me run away or hide. He helped me face the problems head on.

You may believe you're the only person on earth who feels like you do, but you're not. God will provide a counselor, a trusted friend, or a church leader to help you through the valley of hurt and discouragement. We need people who don't try to "fix" us too quickly, who let us vent our pent-up emotions without correcting or condemning, but who gently and persistently point us to God. In a strong, supportive relationship, we can make genuine progress and find the wisdom we need to respond to past hurts, present predicaments, and future possibilities.

Pastor George wasn't a hands-off mentor for me. He defended me, counseled me, and coached me in many difficult conversations. And I was able to watch him respond to a bunch of difficult people with incredible skill, genuine love, and plain truth.

Acknowledge the connection between the past and the present.

If we haven't dealt with the pain of the past, the wounds we experience today will be disproportionately hurtful. If you had a broken arm, how hard would someone have to hit it to hurt really badly? Not too hard! In the same way, many of us walk around with "broken" emotions. Even a slight bump on those inflamed, unhealed wounds is excruciatingly painful. We need to deal with the events in our past so we can handle current offenses with wisdom and strength.

How do we know to what extent the past continues to affect us? Take an extended time to pray. Ask God to reveal any events in the past that haven't been healed and resolved. As you reflect quietly, the Spirit will bring to mind faces and events. Those are the hurts you still need to grieve and the people you need to forgive.

Understand your adversaries.

Instead of labeling those who oppose us as "evil" or "heartless" or "fools," we need to step back and learn to respect them as real people. Genuinely evil sociopaths are rare; most imposing people are overreacting to the pain in their own lives. Perhaps they have responded to us out of fear or jealousy, with a disproportionate reaction due to feeling threatened.

In my case, many of the people who opposed the new direction for the church felt deeply threatened by the change. I was taking their harsh remarks very personally, but Pastor George reminded me that they would have responded the same way to *anyone* who proposed a different direction for the church. Instead of looking only at people's reactions to my leadership, I learned (slowly and haltingly) to look underneath and realize the changes rocked their world.

The entrenched religious leaders had responded much the same way to Jesus. The ultimate example of understanding adversaries was when Jesus was hanging on the cross. He looked at the ones who had falsely accused Him and nailed Him there, and He prayed, "Father, forgive them, for they do not know what they are doing" (Luke 23:34). Didn't they know they were killing Him? Yes, but they didn't understand they had completely missed God's purpose for Jesus' living, loving, and dying. Even when they killed Him, Jesus continued to love them.

Make courageous choices.

Butting heads with people evokes one of two reactions: fight or flight. Some of us are fighters; we blow up, get big, and fire our guns at those who oppose us. Others of us, though, are terrified of confrontation. We run away, change the subject, hide behind a newspaper, and hope the problem will go away. Fighters need to make courageous choices to calm down, ask questions, listen, and try to understand instead of winning at all costs. Those who want to flee need to make the hard decision to stay engaged, to stand up to attacks, and to speak truth even when everything in them wants to run and hide.

Fighters need to make courageous choices to calm down, ask questions, listen, and try to understand instead of winning at all costs. Those who want to flee need to make the hard decision to stay engaged, to stand up to attacks, and to speak truth even when everything in them wants to run and hide.

The choice to forgive is never easy. Our emotions scream for revenge or escape, but forgiveness means we absorb the loss and refuse to harm the person in return. Some people say, "Well, if I forgive when I don't feel like it, I'll be a hypocrite." No, they will be like Jesus. He went to the cross when everything in Him wanted to back away.

Realize that grieving and forgiving are processes, not just events.

At some point we might choose to forgive those who hurt us. But as we face the hurt—especially deep and prolonged hurts like abuse or abandonment—God gradually peels back layers of pain to reveal more damage. At each layer, the offense seems a little clearer and the loss is a little more painful, so with each revelation we must choose to forgive and grieve at a deeper level. That doesn't mean we haven't done the hard work before; it only means we had more to do. This process is entirely normal.

Heal, learn, and grow.

Nobody signs up for a class in facing life's deepest wounds, yet we all find ourselves in this classroom from time to time. When those events happen, we have an opportunity to grow closer to God and gain wisdom we could never acquire any other way. Don't skip class. Don't waste the chance to learn. God can then use you in the lives of others who are suffering and struggling.

Paul assured the Corinthian church that God has a purpose for our pain: "Praise be to the God and Father of our Lord Jesus Christ, the Father of compassion and the God of all comfort, who comforts us in all our troubles, so that we can comfort those in any trouble with the comfort we ourselves receive from God" (2 Corinthians 1:3-4). Our experience of healing gives us credibility and compassion to help others who are suffering.

The cross of Christ changes everything. Human beings simply don't have the innate capacity or motivation to forgive offenses on their own, as seen in the history of warfare and family strife. But when a person experiences the forgiveness of Christ, a heart transformation takes place. Then and only then can we draw from the deep well of love, forgiveness, and unconditional acceptance, and pour those beautiful elements of grace into the lives of those around us. Only then can we love our enemies instead of hating them, or at best, tolerating them. Only then can we pray for those who persecute us or ignore us. Only then can we really imitate the heart of God.

Jesus told a parable about a king forgiving his chief servant the vast sum of 10,000 talents—roughly the equivalent of the gross national product of the three countries surrounding Palestine. The servant, though, wasn't affected by the king's kindness. He immediately went out and choked another servant who owed him a few dollars. When the king heard about the man's hard heart and vicious actions, he called him back in. The king asked him, "Shouldn't you have had mercy on your fellow servant just as I had on you?" (Matthew 18:33) Then the king sent the servant away to be tortured. This is what happens to us when we choose to harbor resentment instead of forgiving. We experience the torture of haunted memories and the poison of planned revenge. Don't let this happen to you. Have mercy on those who have incurred a debt because they have hurt you. Set them free, and in the process, set yourself free.

THINK ABOUT IT...

1. What are some ways we "lose heart" when we butt heads with difficult people?

2. Which of the types of difficult people do you know? (No names, please!) Which ones are easy for you to handle? Which ones drive you nuts?

3. What are some ways bitterness poisons our lives?

4. After reading this chapter, how would you define and describe forgiveness? In what way is it a choice, and in what way is it a process?

5. Which of the suggestions at the end of the chapter seem most helpful to you?

6. As you read this chapter, has the Lord put someone on your heart you need to forgive? Have you realized you need to ask someone to forgive you? What steps are you going to take?

CHAPTER 5

A TALE OF TWO KINGS

Oh, how hard it is to part with power! This one
has to understand.

—Aleksandr I. Solzhenitsyn

Authority has a way of revealing what's in a person's heart. The Bible
has many fascinating stories. One of my favorites is a tale of two kings:
Saul and David.

After the conquest of Canaan, the nation of Israel was a theocracy. Unlike the nations all around them who were ruled by kings, Israel had
designated priests and judges to implement God's laws and purposes.
But as the people looked at the neighboring nations, they decided a
theocracy wasn't for them. They too wanted a king. God agreed to grant
their request, but He let them know they were making a dumb choice.

JEALOUSY AND LOYALTY

The first king of Israel was Saul, a tall, handsome, rich man from the
tribe of Benjamin. Saul's career began with a military victory, but it
was tarnished by the king's disobedience to God's clear command. The
prophet Samuel told him:

"You have done a foolish thing. You have not kept the command the Lord your God gave you; if you had, he would have established your kingdom over Israel for all time. But now your kingdom will not endure; the Lord has sought out a man after his own heart and appointed him ruler of his people, because you have not kept the Lord's command" (1 Samuel 13:13-14).

Saul didn't learn from his mistake. He made other serious blunders in leadership, one time even planning to execute his son Jonathan. The young man had attacked and defeated a superior force of enemy soldiers, but had unknowingly disobeyed a foolish order in doing so. The reward for his bravery? His dad planned to kill him!

Finally, God had seen enough. He sent Samuel to the house of Jesse to select one of his sons to become the new king. As Jesse paraded his tall, handsome sons in front of the prophet, the Lord told Samuel, "No, not this one. No, not that one either." After looking at all seven sons but getting a "No" from God each time, Samuel was confused. He asked, "Are these all the sons you have?" (1 Samuel 16:11) Jesse told him there was one more, the youngest, who was out tending the sheep. It was David. His father hadn't even shown him the respect to include him among his sons when the prophet came for a visit.

When David came in from the fields, God confirmed that this was His choice to become the new king. To everyone's surprise, Samuel anointed David as the nation's monarch. But there was a small problem: Saul was still on the throne.

Meanwhile, the powerful Philistines were at war with Israel. They arrayed their forces for battle against God's people, with the two armies on opposite hills on either side of a valley. Jesse's three oldest sons were soldiers, and the father sent David to take food to them. When they boy arrived at the camp, he walked into a chaotic situation.

The Philistines had a champion, a giant named Goliath, so they proposed a fight between their man and someone from Saul's army—winner take all. Goliath stood in the valley shouting insults and threats. No one from Saul's army had the guts to face the nine-and-a-half-foot mountain of a man until David arrived and immediately volunteered to fight. Saul offered the boy his armor, but it didn't fit, so David took it off.

David grabbed his sling and a few rocks, and he marched into the valley. With one swing of his arm, David flung a rock that hit the giant in the forehead. Goliath was dead when he hit the ground. A boy with a rock saved Saul's army! It was an amazing act of courage. All of Saul's soldiers had pledged their loyalty to the king and his cause, but at a crucial moment of danger, their courage had failed them. David was an innocent bystander. No one expected him to fight the giant, but he stepped up and killed him. His loyalty—to God and to Saul—were unmatched that day.

After David killed Goliath and the Philistines ran from the battlefield, the people sang a new song: "Saul has slain his thousands, and David his tens of thousands." David's courage had rescued Saul, Israel's army, and the entire nation from destruction, but the king couldn't stand that David received so much praise. Scripture tells us, "Saul was very angry; this refrain galled him. . . . And from that time on Saul kept a jealous eye on David" (1 Samuel 18:8-9).

David proved his loyalty beyond a shadow of a doubt, but Saul couldn't see the young man's heart. Jealousy distorted his vision. From that point, the king didn't trust anything David said or did. Saul's twisted perception turned a loyal friend into an enemy.

Jealousy opened the door to demonic oppression in Saul's heart. The next day, an evil spirit came upon him. While David played a harp to entertain his king, Saul grabbed a spear and hurled it at him! This happened twice. I don't know if David was so stunned that he sat there while the king reloaded, or if the second spear was thrown while David ran for his life. The point is that Saul was deadly serious about getting rid of his perceived rival.

In another attempt to get the boy out of his sight, Saul sent David on a mission leading a thousand men. Saul was sure he could have some peace—and maybe David would be killed. But David and his men won great military victories, so the people sang praises even louder. Saul was really peeved now, and even more, he became afraid of David's power, skill, and popularity. He realized the Spirit of God was on this young man.

Before long, Saul considered David such a threat that he tried to catch him and kill him. David gathered a group of men and fled to the desert. Saul and his army relentlessly pursued the renegades. Several times, David and his men narrowly escaped. But on two occasions, David had ideal opportunities to kill Saul, yet he let him walk away. David was so loyal that he wouldn't even harm a man who had sworn to kill him.

David's courage and skill won the hearts of his men. At one point, David made an off-handed comment that he would like a drink of water from a particular well. Three of his men risked their lives to sneak into enemy territory to draw water from the well for David. When they brought it back, David was overwhelmed by their love and loyalty. To honor them, he poured out the water and said, "Is it not the blood of men who went at the risk of their lives?" (2 Samuel 23:13-17)

Before long the Philistines attacked again. This time David wasn't in Saul's army, and Israel was defeated. Saul was wounded, but was not willing to be taken alive. He asked a servant to kill him, but the servant had too much respect for God's anointed king. Saul didn't want to be captured, tortured, and mocked by the cruel Philistines, so he fell on his sword and died. Finally, David became the new king.

Like Saul, those who throw spears of jealousy may eventually fall on their own swords.

Like Saul, those who throw spears of jealousy may eventually fall on their own swords.

When Spears Come at Us

People in authority—parents, bosses, pastors, husbands, or anyone above us on the pecking order—have the power to either build up or tear down, to affirm or destroy. David's relationship with his "mighty men" was an example of good and godly authority. Those men loved each other. David loved them, and they knew it. They were willing to bleed and die to protect him, and they had each other's backs. But Saul threw spears at his most loyal lieutenant.

Few of us have objects literally thrown at us by those in authority, but we get hit by ridicule, sarcasm, unjust criticism, gossip, slander, and many other "slings and arrows of outrageous fortune." We may be able to dodge many of those intangible missiles, but some hit their mark. Talk about a collision! Our dreams and desires get pinned to the wall!

David was under Saul's authority when the king threw spears at him, so he didn't retaliate. He protected himself, but he didn't plot revenge; he wouldn't even take advantage of easy opportunities to harm the man who was his avowed adversary.

When authority figures fling harmful words at us in a staff meeting, we are sometimes tempted to throw back some harsh words of our own. Or perhaps we're more subtle: Rather than confront the person face to face, we undermine his or her authority by questioning decisions in conversations with others. We may "forget" to complete an important job on time, or we delight when the person makes a mistake. In churches, we wear masks of "nice Christians" while we gossip about the one making decisions.

How do we keep our hearts right when a boss, spouse, or pastor treats us with contempt? How do we keep our hearts focused on God when we feel unjustly condemned or overlooked? We have a choice: Be like Saul or be like David. We can react with jealousy, pride, self-pity, and anger, or we can trust God and respond with a beautiful blend of strength, wisdom, and humility.

When spears are thrown at us, we choose to avoid returning fire. We find the right time and the right way to honestly talk about the situation. When we finally find the courage to speak up, we don't blame, lose control, or demand a certain response. (Of course, if laws have been broken and we've been abused in any way, we need to seek legal and police protection, but those situations are relatively rare.) We respond with humility and offer ideas for a solution. No matter how the authority figure reacts, we keep calm—not getting big or getting little.

When we are the ones in authority, David is again our example. Even under the most severe stress any of us can imagine—unjust condemnation, jealousy, and the threat of death—David created an environment that brought out the best in others. He loved his men, and they thrived under his leadership. They admired him, and he responded with reciprocal respect. Together, they faced incredible dangers. The psalmist summarizes David's leadership talents: "And David shepherded them with integrity of heart; with skillful hands he led them" (Psalm 78:72).

Even under the most severe stress any of us can imagine—unjust condemnation, jealousy, and the threat of death—David created an environment that brought out the best in others.

A DAVID IN MY LIFE

When I was 19, soon after Kim and I had married, we attended a service to hear Pastor J. Don George speak. I was very impressed with his knowledge of the Scriptures, his obvious leadership abilities, and his faithfulness to serve in one church for so many years. A few months later, I called to request an appointment to see him. I was just a kid, and I didn't expect to get an audience with such a distinguished leader, so I was surprised when his assistant immediately set up a time for us to meet. A couple of days later I went to his office and told him, "Pastor George, I want to become your right-hand man. I want to go where you go and help you do whatever God has put on your heart. Will you let me serve you this way?"

I realized my request was entirely presumptuous. Dozens of young men would have given their right arms to be Pastor George's assistant, but God had put it on my heart to pursue it. As soon as I got the request out of my mouth, he answered, "Ben, I'd love for you to join me. When can you start?"

One of the reasons I was so attracted to Pastor George is that he's much like my father. Both of them have the highest integrity and authenticity. What they say in public is backed up by their private lives. They don't just tell people to care for others; they sacrifice to help them, all day every day. They love God's Word and teach it with skill and passion. Both of them have earned my love and loyalty. I've known and served Don George for almost twenty years. It's been one of the great pleasures of my life. I'm rich today because of his influence on me. Like David, he's a king worth following.

From the time I was a young man until now as a not-so-young man, Pastor George has always defended me in public. In private, he pointed out my flaws many, many times, but always with the gentleness of a loving dad. He has a remarkable ability to encourage people as he corrects them. Many times I went into a meeting knowing he disapproved of something I had said or done. He spoke honestly and bluntly about the failure, but by the time I walked out, I felt like a million bucks. I never felt demeaned by condemnation or manipulated by praise. He spoke the truth in love, and my spirit grew by leaps and bounds.

As a young pastor I often tried to be funny by making sarcastic comments in my sermons, some of which hurt people who were listening. Pastor George never let things simmer for long. He dealt with problems quickly. A few days later when we were on the road or at his ranch, he would bring it up. He'd say, "Ben, there's something I want to talk about." He described the event and helped me understand how I had hurt people instead of helping them. He always assumed I only wanted to help people, so his tone was never harsh. He would suggest, "Next time, you might say it this way." And we would talk about how God could use the point to build people up. After we finished talking about it, he never brought it up again. He didn't carry a "poop list" to keep track of my faults and flaws. He communicated only grace, hope, and love.

Pastor George often spoke God's vision of the future into my life.

Pastor George often spoke God's vision of the future into my life. I remember a meeting when thirty members of the church staff were gathered. I was twenty-four years old at the time. Pastor George went around the room speaking into each person's life. When he came to me, he said, "Ben Dailey. My vision in life is to raise up ten sons who will build greater churches than anything God has used me to build. Ben will be one of those sons. He will pastor a church that is bigger than our church."

Something happened in my heart at that moment. When he spoke those words about the future, God confirmed His vision for my life. Pastor George's words were prophetic, and they were stunning. He saw something in me that I couldn't detect. God gave him insight into my heart and my future, and he had the boldness to speak the words God gave him. That's what a father does for his child. He unlocks and unleashes talents and dreams the child can't see in himself. Almost twenty years later, I'm living the fulfillment of Pastor George's vision.

Today, Calvary Church is growing. Sometimes people ask, "Do you think Pastor George is jealous of the success of Calvary since you've become the Lead Pastor?"

I almost laugh. They must not know the man at all. I tell them, "There's no one on earth more thrilled with what God's doing than Pastor George. It's the answer to his prayers and the fulfillment of his dreams. Jealous? No way. He's overjoyed."

I have only known two men in my lifetime who don't seem to be threatened by anyone or anything. My dad and Don George are unflappable. Pastor George handles adversity and ridicule with the utmost grace. He never flares up in anger (though I'm sure he's honest with God about his feelings), and he never secretly demeans anyone who has spoken out against him.

I've watched a lot of leaders in my lifetime, and I've come to a conclusion: The only difference between a good leader and great leader is pain tolerance. Great leaders can endure more pain without becoming sidetracked or disheartened. Pastor George doesn't allow setbacks to color the future. He always keeps his eyes on the bigger picture. He believes God will use every success and every failure to accomplish His divine purposes, so there's no need to get downcast when we hit bumps in the road. To me, those bumps seem like tragedies and enormous obstacles, but he's seen it all before. He knows we'll survive, and we'll learn from every difficulty.

However, that is not to say that he is stoic about setbacks. He keeps his heart fixed on the future, but he fully grieves every loss along the way. At times a family might leave the church, and he would say, "Ben, come on. Let's go get an ice cream cone." We sat and discussed our regret about the loss of the family over our cones. When we were finished, he announced, "Okay, let's go." We were finished grieving, and we moved on to tackle the next opportunity God had given us.

Pastor George has an enormous vision, but he never overlooks the small steps it takes to achieve it. He often says, "Details determine destiny." Along with his unusual blend of leadership traits, he empowers people to fulfill their dreams. People know he believes in them and expects the best from them. He enflames godly passion, shapes people's direction, and then launches them with the resources they need to make their goals a reality. He has the uncanny knack of pulling potential out of people. They may be confused, but he helps them clarify their direction, and then he becomes their biggest cheerleader.

He enflames godly passion, shapes people's direction, and then launches them with the resources they need to make their goals a reality.

Even throughout the most sweeping visions and grand plans, he reminds other leaders to remember how the people in the pews will interpret and internalize their message. He wants us to stretch people's faith, but not to the breaking point. He wants us to comfort them, but not leave them too comfortable. The call of Jesus is the most challenging and inspiring message the world has ever heard. Pastor George asks leaders to live in the balance of those twin motivations.

At no time in my relationship with Pastor George did I ever feel he was using me to promote his own success. Far from it. At every point, he has been a father, brother, mentor, shepherd, protector, and friend. He cares about me more than my production. Throughout our relationship, he has advised me to make Kim a priority. He often asked me about our marriage. He encouraged me to take her out on dates and make her feel like a treasure—which she is. He bought me my first black suit. (Every pastor needs at least one!) He also helped me purchase my first car and first little house.

Pastor George has taught me incredible lessons in communication and leadership. I've learned from his verbal input and personal attention, but I've learned even more by watching him. Most people don't see him behind the scenes, but he privately pours out his heart and his time to care for people in trouble. When church leaders fall, many people tend to stand back and criticize them, but not Don George. He gets on a plane and visits them in their home . . . or even in prison. He lets them know they may be fallen, but they are not forgotten. Few people know about his ministry of restoration that has touched the lives of dozens of leaders and their families. He seldom mentions where he's going or where he has been, but I've been close enough to see his compassion in action.

For twenty years, Pastor George has been a second father to me. I have said that we live in a culture of functional orphans, but I'm not one of them. I have two fathers who mean more to me than anyone can imagine. Pastor George has earned my deepest respect and love. I'd do anything for him—not out of any sense of compulsion or fear, but because I want to honor the man I love so much.

I am where I am today because of Pastor George. Many years after I met him and asked if I could serve as his assistant, he told me "the rest of the story." He had agreed so quickly to my request for a very good reason. As Kim and I sat in the service of more than four thousand people, he had seen us out in the crowd. At that moment, the Holy Spirit spoke to him, "When they come to you, I want you to make them a son and daughter to you in the ministry." From the day I started serving him, I knew I was in a favored place, but for years I didn't know the backstory.

Like David's mighty men who were passionately devoted to him because he earned their affection and loyalty, I want ever fiber of my being to honor Don George. It's the highest privilege of my life to know him and serve him. I want his latter years to be even greater than his former years.

But I have associated with other leaders who weren't like Don George.

MORE LIKE SAUL

I've had the opportunity to work with many leaders, and I'm grateful for that privilege. Some have encouraged me and allowed me to flourish, but others competed with me. Working with them seemed like a prison sentence. In every situation, though, I learned valuable lessons.

I remember one leader in particular; I'll call him Mark. A relationship quickly formed as soon as we were introduced. I opened my heart to him, and later I was given the opportunity to serve with him. At first I enjoyed our interaction and learned a great deal from him. Soon, however, I began noticing some inconsistencies in Mark, which weren't hard to spot.

As I spent time working with Mark, I began to realize that although he supported me in private, he often undermined me in public when evaluating a project, a person, or a plan.

FBI agents trained to detect counterfeit bills spend almost all their time looking at actual currency. When they know what the real thing looks like, they can easily spot a fake. I had been close to my dad and Don George for many years, so when it came to ministry, I had seen the real thing every day. As I spent time working with Mark, I began to realize that although he supported me in private, he often undermined me in public when evaluating a project, a person, or a plan. At first, I assumed I had misunderstood, but I quickly realized my hearing wasn't defective. If anyone questioned him about the direction of the ministry, he told them, "I'm not really sure what Ben's doing. He's got some crazy ideas. I'm as frustrated as you are." Pastor George had defended me; Mark left me uncovered.

People soon began looking at me with suspicion. After all, a pastor—a man of God—told them I couldn't be trusted. Very few came to me to clear things up. The rest believed him and took sides. Virtually all of the church was against me. It was just like David and Saul. I was fighting hard and playing my harp with all my might, but Mark was throwing spears at me! At least, that's how it felt.

I tried to be a good team player, but it proved very difficult. I would often tell Mark about an idea for outreach or some other project. We would discuss it and agree on a direction, but the next thing I knew, he changed the story and took all the credit.

I sat down with Mark several times to talk about things I'd heard and the divisions I saw. Each time, he blew me off, telling me, "Ben, I had to say that. This family has been with me from the beginning. They don't understand what you're doing, and I'm trying to empathize with their confusion. Don't worry about it. Just trust me."

Trust him? Day after day, I felt like I was being thrown under the bus—then backed over several times! We had started a journey based on friendship, hope, and vision, but now it felt like I was the target of a terrorist campaign. Instead of being partners on the same team, it felt like a competition, and it broke my heart. In Mark's communication with me, there was never any affirmation or encouragement. He obviously felt threatened and jealous, hoarding any praise for himself.

Eventually the Lord redirected Kim and me, steering us in a new ministry direction. At that point Mark's hurtful, destructive behavior escalated. He implemented a vendetta of innuendo and accusations against me. He told people we were leaving because we had selfish motives and were completely out of God's will. Kim and I were grouped with former staff members who had "stepped out of God's will." Mark said that God had given them sickness and calamities, insinuating they had brought judgment on themselves by rebelling against God's will. He implied that God would judge Kim and me for leaving, too. I tried to explain that we only wanted to be obedient to God's leading, but Mark snarled, "You're only looking for more money!"

When his accusations didn't change my mind, he tried another tactic. He had leaders meet with Kim, attempting to get her to convince me to change my decision. It wasn't enough that he was driving a wedge between the congregation and me; he tried to drive one between Kim and me.

Working with Mark was one of the supreme tests of my life. I felt attacked, betrayed, and belittled, but I was determined to end our time together without regrets.

Working with Mark was one of the supreme tests of my life. I felt attacked, betrayed, and belittled, but I was determined to end our time together without regrets. I really *wanted* to retaliate, but that would only escalate the hatred and suspicion. There had to be another way. Peter wrote that Christ is our example in times of suffering:

> But if you suffer for doing good and you endure it, this is commendable before God. To this you were called, because Christ suffered for you, leaving you an example, that you should follow in his steps. . . . When they hurled their insults at him, he did not retaliate; when he suffered, he made no threats. Instead, he entrusted himself to him who judges justly (1 Peter 2:20-21, 23).

To our best ability, Kim and I kept entrusting ourselves to Him who judges righteously. Many times, Kim told me, "Ben, let's keep our hearts right." We couldn't make Mark become an honorable person, but we could make the hard choice to act honorably. If I hadn't seen Pastor George respond in faith to criticism, I don't know if I could have done it. It was easy to recognize the counterfeit leader, but it was incredibly hard to avoid retribution. Jesus said, "Love your enemies." Mark made himself my enemy. It was my task to dig deep into God's grace to find love for him. Loving him didn't mean I let him abuse me. I spoke up often to confront his lies and challenge his manipulation, but I tried to always speak calmly and with the hope God would use my words to work in his heart.

Kim and I committed to not only honor Mark face to face, but also behind his back. When people began to sense that the situation seemed "off," we never spoke negatively about him. It wasn't easy. It took every ounce of effort and discipline, but we deliberately and consciously chose to speak highly of our leader in the hope that in the future our own staff would do the same for us. I was also reminded of my own shortcomings. (And believe me, I have a long list of my own. I'm not perfect.) Jesus never gave up on me; I shouldn't give up on Mark. Still, it was an unhealthy situation, and God was calling us go a different direction, regardless of whatever opposition we faced. It was time to leave. Since that time, I've forgiven Mark and truly want the best for him. I can forgive only because I've been forgiven much.

BEING LIKE DAVID

Even when Saul threw spears, David refused to hate him. Even when the king chased David in the desert, the young man refused to retaliate. He defended himself and his men, but he didn't take any action to kill "the Lord's anointed." David was willing for God to be the ultimate judge in Saul's life. Eventually, the king took his own life, and David took the throne. He didn't win it by bloodshed, and he didn't manipulate the system. He waited for God to open the door.

The writer to the Hebrews gave clear instructions:

> Remember your leaders, who spoke the word of God to you. Consider the outcome of their way of life and imitate their faith. . . . Have confidence in your leaders and submit to their authority, because they keep watch over you as those who must give an account. Do this so that their work will be a joy, not a burden, for that would be of no benefit to you (Hebrews 13:7, 17).

He doesn't say to submit to a leader's authority only if he's honorable or perfect. We submit because we have confidence our leaders will answer to God. It's far easier and more pleasant to submit to Pastor George, but God used my time with the unreasonable, jealous leader to draw me closer and develop deeper dependence on the Spirit. Submission doesn't mean passivity or apathy. We wade in to the relationship, speaking truth with grace, offering a path for the future, and trusting that God will ultimately have His way, even if we don't see immediate progress.

But of course, we shouldn't be stupid. Suppose a leader is involved in gross sin—immorality, embezzlement, or others—and he wants you to stay quiet. No. You have the responsibility before God to confront the person. Paul was very clear: "Brothers and sisters, if someone is caught in a sin, you who live by the Spirit should restore that person gently. But watch yourselves, or you also may be tempted" (Galatians 6:1).

Our Christian leaders are "brothers and sisters" who sometimes need reproof. Later in life, even David needed someone to point out his sin before God. The prophet Nathan played that role. He confronted David about his sins of adultery and murder. In response, the king responded and repented.

We can't forget that David wasn't alone while he ran from Saul. God gave him a group of men who supported him, loved him, fought by his side, and bled for him. When we're under a leader like Saul, we won't make it if we don't have some mighty men and women by our side. With them, responding in faith can still be difficult and demanding, but without them, it's virtually impossible. Many people wilt, emotionally and spiritually, because they feel isolated and oppressed under insecure leaders.

All of us are under authority. Even a business entrepreneur who is on the top of his company's organizational chart is responsible to his board, and perhaps his shareholders. Senior pastors are responsible to their leadership team, elders, deacons, or some other governing board in the church. For most of us, the line of authority is clear. We answer to a boss, a manager, a government agency, the police, a parent, or a spouse. We need to check our hearts to see how much we line up with David.

Too often we make a sport of finding fault with our leaders. Employees delight in criticizing their bosses. Church members nitpick every word in the sermon and every decision the pastor makes. The closer the relationship, the more painful the ridicule and criticism. Finding fault and spreading gossip aren't spiritual gifts . . . unless we count demons as spirits.

It's possible to have our hearts right in any situation, including conflicts and disagreements. Adolescents are hardwired to pull away from their par-

Finding fault and spreading gossip aren't spiritual gifts . . . unless we count demons as spirits.

ents, but the process doesn't have to be hurtful. In marriages, Paul tells us to submit to one another. Then he tells husbands to love their wives "as Christ loves the church," and he instructs wives to respect their husbands.

Responding in faith to an authority figure can be one of life's greatest challenges. Even if it's difficult—or maybe, *especially* when it's difficult—we can follow the example of Christ and entrust ourselves to the Father who is loving and just. If we genuinely want to honor the Lord, we'll find a way to honor those in authority over us. We may disagree, and we may speak out, but we never demand, condemn, or plot behind their backs.

Even when spears are thrown at us, we never throw them back.

THINK ABOUT IT...

1. What are some possible reasons David didn't retaliate against Saul when the king threw spears and later tried to kill him in the desert?

2.   Who is the most honorable, loving authority figure you've ever
     known? How did that person shape your life?

3.   Have you ever been under a leader like Saul? What kind of ma-
     nipulation or condemnation did the person use? How did he or
     she affect you? How did you respond?

4.   What does it mean for us to "entrust ourselves to God who
     judges righteously"? What peace and confidence does this give
     us?

5. What are some ways you can fulfill the directives in Hebrews 13:7, 17 in your relationship with those in authority over you?

6. What are some lessons we can learn when we choose to respond in faith to difficult leaders? Are those lessons worth the heartache and strain? Why or why not?

CHAPTER 6
EVERYONE, EVERYWHERE

We've drifted away from being fishers of men
to being keepers of the aquarium.

—Paul Harvey

Even a casual reading of the Gospel accounts of the life of Christ immediately reveals a stunning fact: Jesus genuinely loved people others despised. He wasn't putting on a show, and they weren't just projects to Him. He enjoyed hanging out with them! The Pharisees were outraged that He loved Samaritans and tax collectors, confused that He gave attention to women and children (who were considered little more than property at the time), and furious that He healed people on days they considered off limits. (You'd think the miracles would give Him some street cred.)

Today, rigidly religious people must be reading the Pharisees' version of the Bible. They miss Jesus' heart for our society's outcasts, misfits, and others who are often overlooked. If we're not careful, we can miss Jesus' heart, too.

People have a natural tendency to draw boundary markers. We have an innate sense of who's in and who's out, who's acceptable and who should be rejected, who contributes to our success and happiness and who is an annoyance. We prefer people who look like us, believe like us, dress like us, and talk like us. Even the slightest differences can threaten us and ring alarm bells. I've seen people square off and almost come to blows about the times worship services are held and how bulletins are folded. When it comes to music in worship services, some become enraged!

I've talked to people who wonder if a Democrat could actually be a born-again Christian, and I've talked to Democrats who think Republicans escaped from the slimy pit of hell—or maybe didn't escape. And those are the views of Christians!

Outside the warm, loving, grace-filled confines of God's church, two people who both love democracy rant and rave at each other about differences in politics. Republicans despise Democrats for being "soft on defense" and "giving handouts to the poor." Democrats condemn Republicans for not caring about labor unions, the plight of immigrants, and those who don't have healthcare. I've talked to people who wonder if a Democrat could actually be a born-again Christian, and I've talked to Democrats who think Republicans escaped from the slimy pit of hell—or maybe didn't escape. And those are the views of Christians!

I'm tempted to use Rodney King's famous line. After the acquittal of police accused of beating him in an incident that led to riots in Los

Angeles, he said, "People, I just want to say, you know, can we all get along?" The fact is, we can't—at least, not if we're left to human nature. We need something more, something deeper. We need our hearts to collide with God's so they can be marvelously changed.

THE BEAUTY OF DIVERSITY

When a body of Christians doesn't reflect its community, something's wrong. When Pastor George started our church, Irving was overwhelmingly white. Over several decades, the demographics of Irving and the surrounding area changed, but the church didn't. Pastor George realized something drastic needed to happen. The church was too white, and it had become too old. He asked me to come in to change the equation. That's when the sparks started flying!

As I described in an earlier chapter, we took bold steps to broaden our boundary markers to include people from different races, cultures, ages, worship styles, socioeconomic classes, and nationalities. Some people felt terribly threatened by the influx of "those people." A lot of them simply couldn't handle it, and they left. Those who stayed have enjoyed the rich textures and colors of diversity. Our church is a far more vibrant place today than it has ever been. From the beginning of the transition, we didn't want to barely push the markers out. We wanted to blow them down! We didn't want to tolerate diversity; we wanted to celebrate it. And we do.

I can imagine the look on Jesus' face when social outcasts of all kinds gathered around Him: lepers, blind, lame, crippled, children, foreigners, adulterers, prostitutes, and tax gatherers. I'm sure He was thrilled. He delighted in their presence. I can also imagine the expression on His face when the scowling Pharisees walked toward Him. He was pained by their rigid rejection of the people God loves. Paul told the Ephesians,

"Do not grieve the Holy Spirit of God" (Ephesians 4:30). The arrogance of the Pharisees grieved the Holy Spirit. I didn't want our church to grieve God by our exclusion of people He loves—*any* people He loves.

We can be very creative in our capacity to exclude others. We can be snobs about the superiority of our race, our politics, our theology, our social circle, our football team, or the fact that we don't smoke, drink, and cuss like "those people." The Gospels tell us the Pharisees were shocked that Jesus even ate with "sinners," which was a sign of genuine acceptance in that culture.

In *The Call*, Os Guinness notes, "Exclusiveness and exclusion always result from making a false idol of purity. Pharisaism, in fact, is the result of a perverted passion for theological purity just as ethnic cleansing is for racial purity."[22]

I know what it means to be a religious snob. I grew up in a Baptist church that looked down on the Southern Baptists because we thought they were too liberal! My dad's church grew because he consistently preached grace, but most of the others in the fellowship of independent churches remained small. Why? Because what they considered "commitment to preaching the hard truth" was actually angry condemnation. Our denomination was proud of the fact that we were superior to "those churches," and we regularly passed judgment on "those Christians" who weren't as committed, as obedient, or as right as we were. We were card-carrying, first-class religious snobs.

In my family, the standing joke is, "Ask me what I'd be if I wasn't a Baptist."

---

22 Os Guinness, *The Call* (Nashville: Thomas Nelson, 1998), p. 108.

"Okay, what would you be?"

"I'd be ashamed of myself."

The Baptists, though, don't have a corner on religious bigotry. People who belong to the Assemblies, Methodists, Presbyterians, Catholics, and everybody else can draw boundaries around their uniqueness and feel superior to those outside the circle. When we consider differences, we don't say, "We disagree on a few things, but we find common ground on many points." Instead, we focus on the points of disagreement and conclude, "We're right and you're wrong—so wrong that you're disqualified!"

People can only belong to our group if they ascribe to the narrow, prescribed set of beliefs, practices, clothes, and life- **Pastor George taught me to be a gracist** style. Those who don't toe the line are the targets of **instead of a racist.** sideways glances and gossip—and maybe outright ridicule. And if a person actually had a tragic failure like a divorce or a DUI, the game was over! That person was branded with the scarlet letter: L for *loser*. If you think that's an exaggeration, you weren't at Calvary when we went through "the change," and you haven't been in any hardcore religious or political organizations lately.

Pastor George taught me to be a *gracist* instead of a *racist*. His godly inclusion, though, goes far beyond the color of a person's skin. His attitude, like Christ's, is: "No matter who you are, no matter what you've done, no matter what you wear, no matter what you can give, no matter what you need from us, we love you and accept you just like you are." That's my mantra, too. If we fail, let it be on the side of grace, not judgment. We'd rather be criticized for loving too much than loving too little.

I believe we relate to three kinds of people: those who are like us, those who are unlike us, and those who oppose us. We naturally gravitate to those who are like us. We have enough problems loving them, but we need them as allies against the other two groups. In fact, we often define our group's boundary markers by identifying people and causes we're against. People who join political groups may have little in common except their commitment to defeat an opposing candidate. Every policy on our side is good and right, and everything the other party supports is stupid and evil.

Many people who are unlike us aren't even on our radar. We drive past them every day without even noticing they exist. A group of immigrants waits in a parking lot every morning, hoping to get jobs as day laborers. We don't wonder if they'll get work today, and we don't consider the impact on their wives and kids if they don't find jobs. They might as well be invisible. The same could be said for elderly people in nursing homes; children in state facilities because their parents are deadbeats, dead, or in jail; homeless people; addicts; those who are mentally ill; refugees who have found asylum in America; sex slaves; and other groups who seldom dent the minds of the average, middle class American. As long as those people stay outside our neighborhoods and our churches, we don't care.

When they get close, however, the game changes. If people of different races, nationalities, or lifestyles buy a house down the street, we become outraged because we fear our property values will go down. If they come to our churches, we look down our noses at them because they don't measure up to our standards. They have always been outside our boundary markers. When they push inside, we don't like it one bit!

A young woman came to our church wearing a short skirt and a halter-top, and some of the women almost blew a gasket. One of them snarked, "What if my daughter saw her? What kind of influence is she?"

I told her, "Maybe your daughter would care enough to look beyond her clothes and realize she may have walked in the door because God is at work to open her heart to His love. Maybe, just maybe."

One day at the airport I noticed a sign that read, "Smoking Area." A group of people was in the small room, puffing away. I realized the world sends a message to people who smoke: "If you want to smoke, don't leave. We'll make a place for you." Why couldn't the church do as much to welcome smokers? When our people bring friends who smoke, some may get nervous because they haven't been in church in a long time. When they get fidgety, they want a cigarette. If they walk out to the parking lot to smoke, they may never walk back in, so we wanted to provide a safe, welcoming place in the middle of our campus to show them a little love. We didn't promote it, but we didn't make it uncomfortable for smokers to attend our church. We simply removed one more barrier for people who might be interested in hearing the gospel.

One man almost shouted in anger, "What's next, a pole for strippers?"

Predictably, some regular attendees went ballistic when they found out about our plans to have a smoking area at the church. One man almost shouted in anger, "What's next, a pole for strippers?" Another snarled,

"If we're going to give people what they want, we might as well serve whiskey." A lady told me, "I can't believe you're going to let my kids see people smoking!" Does she keep her children locked up in a closet? If they go out at all, they see people smoking. I guess the church members who were so adamant against our smoking area haven't read the Bible passages about sinners flocking to Jesus because they felt completely welcomed and loved.

It's no wonder many who are outside the church don't want to have anything to do with the Christian faith. Their hesitation isn't about Jesus. When we ask them what they think of Christ, they say He's loving, kind, powerful, and gracious. They may not be able to tell you where the stories of miracles are found in the Bible, but most of them can recount a few examples of Christ's healing power. They have great respect for Jesus, but they feel ridiculed and rejected by His fan club.

Mahatma Gandhi was a leader for independence and human rights in India in the twentieth century. He was a Hindu, but he had plenty of interaction with Christians. His observations were similar to those of the people in neighborhoods throughout our country. He said, "I like your Christ. I do not like your Christians. They are so unlike your Christ."[23] When John the Baptist was in prison and about to be executed, he sent his disciples to Jesus to be sure He was the Messiah. There's nothing like impending death to force us to be sure about the most important things in life. Jesus sent back word to John that, yes, He was the one everyone had been waiting for, and His miracles proved it. When John's messengers left, Jesus turned to His followers and told them about the greatness of John. Then He told them, "From the days of John

---

23 Cited by Dan Kimball, Margaret Feinberg, *They Like Jesus But Not the Church, Participant's Guide* (Grand Rapids: Zondervan, 2008), p. 7.

the Baptist until now, the kingdom of heaven has been subjected to violence, and violent people have been raiding it" (Matthew 11:12).

What was the source of violence against Jesus? It was twofold: religious and political factions. The Pharisees and Sadducees objected to Jesus' message and plotted to kill Him. We see them trying to refute Jesus, twisting His words, and demanding signs. Over and over again, the masses of people flocked to hear Him speak, see His miracles, and feel His touch, but the angry religious elite despised the Lord of life.

The other source of opposition was the political elite. Herod Antipas had John arrested, and soon he would cut off the baptist's head. That's opposition! In most churches, political opposition isn't a problem, but the religious elite feels threatened by change, by inclusion, and by love. They claim to be doing God's will, but they fight tooth and nail against the open arms and loving heart of Jesus.

In most churches, political opposition isn't a problem, but the religious elite feels threatened by change, by inclusion, and by love. They claim to be doing God's will, but they fight tooth and nail against the open arms and loving heart of Jesus.

Do you think this criticism is too harsh? If you do, you haven't been the recipient of letters and emails like I've received, and you haven't seen the hatred in people's eyes like I've seen. Whenever we broaden our boundaries to reach out to more people, some at the center feel threatened, and they lash out in anger.

But there's another way to understand the last part of Jesus' statement. Who are the "violent" who take the kingdom of God "by force"? They are the outcasts who feel so loved and accepted they can't wait to get in! They break down any walls—culturally, relationally, and emotionally—to enter the Kingdom so they can experience the kindness and healing power of God. They're so thirsty for living water that they break the carefully established protocols to get in and have a drink. This creates a collision of cultures—the rigid vs. the flexible; exclusion vs. inclusion. When the rush of the Spirit makes hearts brand new, nothing can contain them. Some people, though, try to cling to old ways, with disastrous results.

Jesus told a parable to illustrate this point:

> "No one tears a piece out of a new garment to patch an old one. Otherwise, they will have torn the new garment, and the patch from the new will not match the old. And no one pours new wine into old wineskins. Otherwise, the new wine will burst the skins; the wine will run out and the wineskins will be ruined. No, new wine must be poured into new wineskins. And no one after drinking old wine wants the new, for they say, 'The old is better'" (Luke 5:36-39).

Jesus was saying that we can't mix the old covenant of the law with the new covenant of grace. In a practical sense, those who cling to rigid, legalistic practices and perspectives (like the Pharisees in Jesus' day and angry, pharisaic people today) can't hold the vibrant, messy ministry of reaching out to new people. New wine needs new wineskins to expand and hold it. A ministry of radical inclusion needs new practices to expand and hold them, too. It makes perfect sense, but it drives some people into a frenzy.

MY NEIGHBOR

One of the most famous dialogues in the Gospels occurred when an expert in the law tried to trick Jesus. It was posed as a simple question, but it was intended as a rhetorical landmine. He asked, "Teacher, what must I do to inherit eternal life?"

Jesus wouldn't take the bait. He asked the man, "What is written in the Law? How do you read it?"

To his credit, the man gave an honest answer. But he stepped on the landmine! He could have articulated all 613 laws enumerated in the Old Testament. If not, which ones would he include, and which would he exclude? If he omitted any, he would be open to fierce condemnation from others in the religious establishment sitting next to him. Instead, he answered, "'Love the Lord your God with all your heart and with all your soul and with all your strength and with all your mind'; and, 'Love your neighbor as yourself'" (Luke 10:27). He didn't list over 600 specific laws, and he didn't name the Big Ten. He responded with one primary law and an addendum: "Love God, and then out of a full heart, love others. The rest is details."

This is one of the most profound—and one of the most misunderstood—passages in the Bible. Most people overlook the first (and more important) command, and they make big mistakes on the other one. They either try to force themselves to muster up enough love for people they don't like, or they give up entirely and feel smug or guilty (depending on their conscience).

Let's unpack Jesus' statement. Our first priority, our greatest challenge and delight, is to have such a deep, wonderful love relationship with God that it affects every fiber of our being.

Our first priority, our greatest challenge and delight, is to have such a deep, wonderful love relationship with God that it affects every fiber of our being.

delight, is to have such a deep, wonderful love relationship with God that it affects every fiber of our being. This kind of love permeates our hearts (emotions, will, and convictions), our souls, (the immaterial part of us), our strength (talents, abilities, and clout), and our minds (reason and thinking). Then, after our hearts are flooded with the wonder of knowing Jesus, His love spills out into the lives of others—our neighbors.

We can care for people in many different ways, two of which are extending mercy and justice. We show mercy to those who are hurting, poor, and suffering. We fight for justice for victims of crime and oppression.

In his insightful book, *Generous Justice*, pastor Tim Keller cites a Harvard professor in making the strong connection between delight in God and involvement in caring for those in need:

> Elaine Scarry of Harvard has written a fascinating little book called *On Beauty and Being Just*. Her thesis is that the experience of beauty makes us less self-centered and more open to justice. I have observed over the decades that when people see the beauty of God's grace in Christ, it leads them powerfully toward justice.[24]

When I see someone who delights in excluding classes of people or individuals, whose anger is more prominent than affection, and who makes a sport of finding fault in others, I conclude that the person isn't filled to overflowing with the love of Jesus. In most cases, the reason why people don't love others is precisely because the love of God hasn't sunk deeply into their own souls. Their anger, superiority, and

24   Tim Keller, *Generous Justice* (New York: Dutton, 2011), p. xx.

condemnation of others come out of a still-desperate, still-wounded heart. The first question, then, is, "Am I delighting in God's magnificent love for me?" And the second is, "Is His love overflowing into the lives of others?"

In the conversation between Jesus and the expert in the law, a problem arose. The lawyer didn't feel comfortable with his own answer. He realized loving his neighbor was too big, too broad, and too much for him. He tried to exclude a bunch of people by asking, "And who is my neighbor?" Jesus had praised him earlier for giving a right answer, but then He followed up with a lesson the religious expert would never forget.

Jesus told a story about a Jewish man who was traveling a dangerous road between Jerusalem and Jericho. Bandits captured him, beat him to a pulp, and robbed him, leaving him half dead. A few minutes later, a priest came along. When he saw the man lying on the side of the road, he was unwilling to help. He walked on by. Similarly, a Levite came along, but he too failed to help the man. Finally, a Samaritan came along. The Samaritans were half-breeds, despised by the Jews. A Jew wouldn't think of stooping to help a Samaritan in trouble, but now the tables were turned.

The Samaritan stopped to care for the Jewish man. He risked his life— he could have been the next victim of the bandits—and he invested his time, money, and attention to help the man. He didn't just flip him a coin and say, "Good luck." He tenderly dressed his wounds, put him on his donkey, took him to an inn, and cared for him all night. The next day, he paid for the man to convalesce for a few more days.

After telling the parable, Jesus asked the lawyer, "Which of these three do you think was a neighbor to the man who fell into the hands of robbers?"

The lawyer said, "The one who had mercy on him."

Jesus concluded, "Go and do likewise" (Luke 10:25-37).

The priest and the Levite thought they had good reasons to keep on going. They didn't know if the man was already dead. If he was and they touched him, they would be ceremonially unclean and couldn't worship in the temple. But isn't that the point? Which do we value more: our nice, clean, orderly, religious lives, or the opportunity to pour out God's love to those in need? Am I more like the two who walked by, or like the Samaritan? How about you?

Which do we value more: our nice, clean, orderly, religious lives, or the opportunity to pour out God's love to those in need? Am I more like the two who walked by, or like the Samaritan? How about you?

The real kicker in the story is that it was a Samaritan who stopped to help and gave so generously to care for the Jewish man. Those who were listening that day must have been shocked. Jesus' story challenges every boundary of race, culture, class, and religion. No one, Jesus is saying, is outside the circle of "neighbor" for any of us. God loves every person on the planet, and if our hearts are filled and overflowing, we will love them too—blacks, whites, Asians, and Hispanics; Democrats and Republicans; hipsters and geeks; those who raise their hands in worship and those who kneel; mansion dwellers and the homeless; straights, gays, and bisexuals. They all are our neighbors.

Are we racists or gracists?

There's a big difference between *favor* and *favoritism*. The Samaritan showed the Jewish man favor when he stopped to give him focused attention

Many people in the church aren't willing to experience even the slightest inconvenience for the sake of others.

and generous care. He had been on his own agenda, but he changed his plans to pour out his time and resources on someone in need. Favoritism is very different. It's purposefully neglecting the needs of the many to accommodate the greed of a few. Favor includes even the most down and out. It's in line with the heartbeat of God. Favoritism thrives on excluding everyone but the up and comers. It knows nothing of God's heart at all.

Many people in the church aren't willing to experience even the slightest inconvenience for the sake of others. They don't want to have to park farther away because so many new people are coming, they don't want to smell those who haven't washed, and they don't want to hear any cursing in the lobby. But the Samaritan wasn't just inconvenienced when he cared for the bandits' victim. He invested himself, his money, his time, and his honor to care for him. His honor? Certainly. How do you think other Samaritans would have viewed his acts of kindness to a hated Jew? They would have blasted him! He risked ridicule from all sides to care for the wounded man.

In our unity, though, we don't lose diversity. Sometimes I hear pastors say, "In our church, we don't see color. Everyone's the same at the foot of the cross." In a way, that's true. No one is superior or inferior, yet coming to Christ doesn't erase our ethnicity and culture.

The picture of the redeemed family of God in heaven shows a rich tapestry of amazing variety. At least three times in his revelation, John mentions this diversity. For example: "After this I looked and there before me was a great multitude that no one could count, from every nation, tribe, people and language, standing before the throne and in front of the Lamb. They were wearing white robes and were holding palm branches in their hands" (Revelation 7:9).

For all of eternity, each culture's expression of true faith will complement and inspire all the others. It will be a beautiful dance and a glorious feast of the family of God. Do we ever sense this appreciation for each other today?

BREAKING THEM DOWN

Some people are temperamentally kind. Such dear people are the first to show up when people experience a tragedy. Their casseroles are terrific! When people of other races, sexual preferences, or economic strata sit near them in church, they at least smile to greet them.

Many more people are like the two men who walked by on the Jericho road. Those people don't want to be bothered by the needs of others. They value their own convenience so highly that they lack concern for another's distress. They try to be the first in line at the cafeteria after church!

They can't imagine having an actual conversation with a lesbian, a homeless person, or someone from India.

Still others are genuinely threatened by change. They fight, kick, and gouge to keep "those people" out. They may give some money to help them, but it's always at arm's length. They can't imagine having an actual conversation with a lesbian, a homeless person, or someone from India. They remind me of the family who sat in my office and told me that they were moving their teenager to another youth group because there were too many ethnicities represented in ours. The dad remarked, "Pastor, I'm sure you understand. We want our daughter to be around other kids who are just like her. You know, if she's around too many black teenagers, well . . . you understand." His sentence trailed off, coupled with a slight smile and nod that suggested I should know what he meant, even if he didn't want to say it—a kind of secret code of arrogant exclusion.

I replied, "No! I *don't* understand!"

Conflict doesn't end by one party walking away, and it isn't over when one person bludgeons another with persuasive arguments (persuasive to him, at least). Too often we try to win at all costs, or we attempt to ignore the problem and hope it will go away.

Paul offers a different solution. In his day, the division between people was exemplified by the racial animosity between Jews and Gentiles. Each group hated the other, despised the other's practices, and was suspicious of every motive. In the temple in Jerusalem, Jewish men could go into the inner sanctuary, but women were kept outside. And even beyond them was an area designated as "the court of the Gentiles." Around this area was a wall to keep non-Jewish people from getting too near the worshiping Jewish men. The wall was the ultimate boundary marker.

Paul wrote to a church that included both Gentiles and Jews, and he gave them a radical solution to the division that always exists:

> The Messiah has made things up between us so that we're now together on this, both non-Jewish outsiders and Jewish insiders. He tore down the wall we used to keep each other at a distance. He repealed the law code that had become so clogged with fine print and footnotes that it hindered more

than it helped. Then he started over. Instead of continuing with two groups of people separated by centuries of animosity and suspicion, he created a new kind of human being, a fresh start for everybody (Ephesians 2:14-15, *The Message*).

How can this happen? What does it take for two groups with polar-opposite backgrounds or opinions come together? We can't just decide to be nice to each other. The old animosities are too strong for that. It takes a powerful force to change our perception and motivation, a power that transforms us from the inside out, turns hatred into love, and provides the desire to embrace those we once considered enemies. Racism, prejudice, and cultural superiority don't end by applying half-measures. It takes something extensive and radical. It takes the cross. Paul tells us:

It takes a powerful force to change our perception and motivation, a power that transforms us from the inside out, turns hatred into love, and provides the desire to embrace those we once considered enemies.

Christ brought us together through his death on the cross. The Cross got us to embrace, and that was the end of the hostility. Christ came and preached peace to you outsiders and peace to us insiders. He treated us as equals, and so made us equals. Through him we both share the same Spirit and have equal access to the Father (Ephesians 2:16-18, *The Message*).

Christ paid the ultimate price to bring each of us back to God. We had been enemies, but in the cross of Christ, God made us His friends—and even better, His children. The sacrifice of Jesus killed the hostility between God and humankind, and when we let it sink into our human relationships, it kills the suspicion and hatred between people.

An African proverb says, "When I saw him from afar, I thought he was a monster. When he got closer, I thought he was an animal. When he got closer still, I realized he is a human. When we got face to face, I realized he is my brother." As long as we let walls separate us from other groups of people, they remain monsters, and we easily dismiss them. We feel completely justified in campaigning against the monsters who threaten us for any reason. We call them names, laugh when they hurt, and rejoice when our side is winning.

When Paul's letter was read in the church, both Jews and Gentiles sat listening. How do you think each group felt? The Jews probably thought, *Good grief. Paul is making those people equal to us!* And the Gentiles probably cheered and danced. Paul was giving them full membership in God's family! They weren't second-class anymore.

How do you and I feel when we read this passage and think about the people who sit near us in church? Do we feel threatened, or do we shout for joy? Our response says a lot about our hearts.

Aside from terrorism and other crimes, the problems between groups of people today aren't primarily matters of race, creed, or culture. It's a heart disease. We don't love God enough, and therefore, we don't have the inner resources to love others very well.

The first step is honesty. We need to think about what we've thought and said about groups of people in the last few days. Do we blame political parties for our problems? Do we complain about "irresponsible poor people" taking too many of our resources or "greedy rich people" not paying enough taxes? Do we fuss and fume when immigrants move in near us, and are we delighted when those we despise lose a legal battle? Do we justify our anger by seeing classes, groups, and races of people as monsters? The more we have tightened our boundary markers more than Jesus did, the more we need to repent.

It's human nature to be restrictive. We don't easily expand our boundaries to include a broad definition of "neighbor." We have plenty of excuses for continuing to exclude classes of people.

Jonathan Edwards was one of the greatest preachers in our nation's history. Before the American Revolution, he was the minister of a church in Massachusetts. His writings and teachings still speak to our hearts today. One of his powerful sermons was titled "The Duty of Charity to the Poor." Edwards identified several common objections Christians raise to excuse them from helping people in need. He said that we often distinguish between the "deserving poor" and those who don't deserve our help.

Those in the first category are the victims of crime, disease, and natural disasters. They suffer through no fault of their own. Those in the second group, though, are different. They're poor because they made bad choices. They have ruined their lives with addictions, thrown their money away on stupid things, committed crimes, and entered the country illegally (among other reasons). Yes, they're suffering, but they brought it on themselves!

In light of the sacrifice of Christ, Edwards saw no distinction between the two groups. He explained, "Christ loved us, and was kind to us, and was willing to relieve us, though we were very hateful persons, of an evil disposition, not deserving of any good . . . so we should be willing to be kind to those who are . . . very undeserving."[25]

Before we ca. change, or open our hearts to love more people, or demonstrate .ie love of God to those who have been outsiders, we have to repent. Repentance is a basic concept in the Bible, and it never loses its significance. When we repent, we turn from sinful attitudes and behaviors and make new choices to honor God. We look our selfish, narrow, judgmental attitudes right in the eye and call them "sin." We don't excuse ourselves, and we don't minimize the suspicion in our hearts. We face it squarely, admit it, and thank God for His wonderful forgiveness.

We look our selfish, narrow, judgmental attitudes right in the eye and call them "sin." We don't excuse ourselves, and we don't minimize the suspicion in our hearts. We face it squarely, admit it, and thank God for His wonderful forgiveness.

The experience of forgiveness is the essential first step in expanding our boundaries. Paul promised the Romans, "Therefore, there is now no condemnation for those who are in Christ Jesus" (Romans 8:1).

The next step is to identify the neighbors we have neglected and make plans to reach out to them. Who are the ones we've spoken harsh words about? We stop saying those things—even if all our friends still use venomous language in talking about them. True repentance changes hearts *and* actions. Like the Samaritan, we notice needs and invest

---

25   Mark Valeri, *Works of Jonathan Edwards, 1730-1733*, vol. 17 (New Haven: Yale University Press, 1999), p. 397.

our resources to meet those needs. The list of possibilities is almost endless: Spend one Saturday each month as a volunteer at a food bank, donate money to dig wells in Africa, stop under a bridge to feed a homeless person, invite a family new to the country to a home-cooked dinner, and stop driving by those in need. Like the Samaritan, our hearts need to be tenderized by the gospel of grace so we care enough to help. We can't help every person every time, but we can sacrifice our own convenience more often to reach a significant number of people.

God smiles when compassion replaces judgment, but we need to channel our compassion so it's effective. A handout isn't the right solution to every problem. We need to use our God-given discernment and wisdom. For instance, giving money to people with sad messages at stop signs may not be the best investment of one's resources, and it may actually hurt more than help. A New York reporter investigated forty such people and discovered that many, if not most, of them used the contributions to buy drugs. A far more effective and compassionate action would be giving the money to an agency that has the training and skill to help addicts get into recovery and provide homeless people with a future. Throwing money at a few needs may soothe our consciences, but it may do more harm than good.

We'll get a lot farther down the road toward inclusion and care if we find a group of people who are actively in the process of reaching out to outcasts and others in need. If a pastor proclaims, "We value diversity," but if no one on the platform has an accent, a youthful appearance, or different color skin, his assurance doesn't carry much weight.

Find a church, a small group, a non-profit organization, or an agency whose work captures your heart, and dive in. You'll probably find the work of caring for outcasts is much messier than you ever imagined, but you'll also find that it's more rewarding than you dreamed possible. No matter how much you invest of your heart, your tears, and your treasure, you'll find that you're tapping into God's expansive, tender heart. That's reward enough.

Eventually we'll get a report card from God. If we've trusted in Christ, we'll avoid the Great White Throne judgment because our names are written in the Book of Life. But there's another day of reckoning for all believers. Someday we'll stand before Jesus to give an account of every attitude and action since the day we trusted Christ (1 Corinthians 3:10-15). On that day, one of the most important measuring sticks will be how we treated the poor and displaced.

Shortly before Jesus went to the cross, He taught His followers some very important lessons. He had told them many times that He was going to be killed. In one parable, He compared himself to a wealthy master who entrusted his wealth to three servants. It was their job to invest the money until the master returned—just like it's our task to invest our time, talents, and treasure for God until Jesus comes back. Then Jesus told a second story. In this one, the king (representing Jesus) told his followers:

> "Come, you who are blessed by my Father; take your inheritance, the kingdom prepared for you since the creation of the world. For I was hungry and you gave me something to eat, I was thirsty and you gave me something to drink, I was a stranger and you invited me in, I needed clothes and you clothed me, I was sick and you looked after me, I was in prison and you came to visit me" (Matthew 25:34-36).

Those listening didn't understand. They asked, "What in the world are you talking about? When did we do all this for you?" (Matthew 25:37-39, Author's paraphrase)

The King answered, "Truly I tell you, whatever you did for one of the least of these brothers and sisters of mine, you did for me" (Matthew 25:40).

Don't miss this crucial truth. It will change how you see the needy people around you—and if it doesn't yank on your heart, you might wonder if you know the heart of Jesus at all. When we turn up our noses at people we consider beneath us, we're turning up our noses at Jesus. When we blast people for their political views or cultural preferences, we're blasting Jesus. When we notice people in need but fail to take risks and invest in helping them, we're neglecting Jesus. But when we notice and reach out to care for "the least of these," it's as if we are attending to Jesus personally. Don't miss this crucial truth. It will change how you see the needy people around you—and if it doesn't yank on your heart, you might wonder if you know the heart of Jesus at all.

In many churches, people major on the minors. They fight about the lamest things. People get their feelings hurt, and they exhaust their energies finding allies and launching attacks. It's so sad . . . and so destructive. When we tap into the heart of God—when our desires collide with His heart and He wins—we won't spend time worrying about things that don't matter. All our energies will be devoted to making a difference, touching lives, and changing the destiny of people in need. We'll care about the causes and people who are on God's heart.

The most exciting times in our church during the past year occurred when we looked beyond our own wants to care for others. The people of Calvary Church donated thousands of bags of groceries to feed people who couldn't afford to provide food for their families. We invited 2,000 single mothers to bring their kids, and we gave those children the gift of their dreams. The looks on the kids' faces made it all worthwhile, but their mothers had the same look.

Last spring my wife was the first of thirteen people in our church to donate a car to a family in need of transportation. We watched family after family overwhelmed by practical and blatant expressions of love. And honestly, I've never seen our people more joy-filled and excited to give. Something incredible happens when God opens our hearts and our wallets, and we make a genuine difference in people's lives. It's a thrill. We can't get enough of it.

It's wonderful to have programs in churches that reach out to disadvantaged people. However, a harder task may be to walk across the street in your neighborhood or down the hall at work to connect with people who are different. In those situations you can't count on the momentum of masses to push you along to do good for others. It's just Jesus and you. We need to trust Him to give us enough love to extend to a loud, obnoxious neighbor, a family from El Salvador who has moved across the street, a coworker who's gay, a yard man who doesn't speak English, a huge guy with tattoos and piercings (like some of the people on my staff), a woman who covers the cuts on her arm, a proud Democrat or a fierce Republican, a friend whose kids are out of control, and countless others. Such people feel "less than" because they're *treated* as "less than"—not only by society at large, but more pointedly, by Christians.

When we see people who are different from us, do we avoid eye contact? Do we give a quick nod, but walk on by? Or do we take the initiative to engage the person in conversation, to find out more so we can care more deeply? And then, do we take the time to build a relationship? Those people are our neighbors, not just "targets for the gospel." They're human beings created and loved by God. They have inherent value because they exist, whether they ever trust in Jesus or not. Will we be good Samaritans?

Many people outside the church have watched us and concluded we're only interested in selling them a commodity—the gospel. They don't want to hear a sales pitch; they want to be loved. Let me assure you, they'll be far more likely to listen to our gospel message if they believe we love them with no strings attached. Authentic love opens hearts. The first step is to be a friend.

Some of us think it's our job to point out people's failures. We assume, "If they feel bad enough, maybe they'll change." Here's a news flash: Most people are well aware of their sins. They don't need us to remind them.

One of my favorite stories in the Gospels is about the Samaritan woman at the well whom Jesus traveled out of His way to meet at the hottest part of the day. She was trying to get her identity from her sexuality, but she had a string of broken dreams behind her. Jesus didn't begin by blasting her. He started by gently and respectfully moving toward her. He asked her for a drink of water. The first point of contact was on her terms. He then got to the heart of things. Rather than seeking meaning and identity in sexual relationships, He said, she could find a more satisfying source of true refreshment through a relationship with Him.

We're familiar with the gospel message Jesus shared with her, but we might miss the incredible expanse of His boundary markers. She was a woman—a second-class citizen in those days. She was a Samaritan—and John makes sure the readers understand: "For Jews do not associate with Samaritans." And she was living in sin, which caused people in her own village to ridicule her so she didn't draw water with the other women early in the morning, but waited until the heat of the day.

Jesus was culturally astute. He knew all those barriers existed, but He didn't care. He waded past them all to extend a hand of grace to a woman who felt like an outsider in her own community. This instance, though, is hardly unique in Jesus' life. Throughout the Gospels, we see Him interacting with outsiders: having dinner with hated tax collectors, blessing children (whom His disciples considered annoyances), and touching lepers, blind people, and those who were demon possessed. Jesus didn't just *say* He loved people. He consistently went out of His way to *show* it.

Jesus didn't just *say* He loved people. He consistently went out of His way to *show* it.

In his book, *Just Walk Across the Room*, pastor Bill Hybels suggests that most of us don't normally rub shoulders with people who are different from us. In fact, we've moved into neighborhoods to get away from all kinds of people we consider undesirable. Now, even when we want to reach out, we're isolated from needy people. To touch them, we have to think hard, plan strategically, and take steps to connect with them in meaningful ways. We can go to restaurants in parts of town we seldom visit, shop at stores and markets on the other side of town, and put ourselves in situations where we make contact with people outside our "circle of comfort."[26] When we go to those places, we can ask God for divine appointments. As we strike up conversations, we may find some as thirsty for God as the Samaritan woman at the well. And if they're not interested in Jesus, at least we've shown them some love.

I challenged people in our church to "get out of the box"—to do anything and everything (just short of sin) to connect with people where they live, work, and play. I encouraged them to go to nursing homes, bars, casinos, playgrounds, and anywhere else people congregate. I told them, "If you'll get out of the box, I'll get *in* the box. If you bring enough people to church to find God's love and connect with this body of believers, I'll stay in a six-by-six-by-six Plexiglas box on the roof of the church overlooking the highway for three days and nights." I threw out this absurd idea after watching a David Blaine special. It was so outlandish I felt pretty safe. I didn't actually believe I might have to make good on my offer.

Our people love a challenge. I set a goal of 8,000 people; they brought 9,000. During the three days and nights I stayed in the box over the highway, people came to see the spectacle. I talked to a lot of them, and I prayed for many people who asked. Meanwhile, the people in our church didn't stay in the parking lot to watch. They went out into the community to serve over 10,000 needy people. In fact, they did some crazy things. Several women went to strip clubs to show the love of Jesus to pole dancers. (A few men wanted to lead this outreach, but rest assured, I only allowed women to be involved.)

One group took makeup and perfume, and they talked with the dancers about their hopes and dreams. Others took napkins with the

---

26 Bill Hybels, *Just Walk Across the Room* (Grand Rapids: Zondervan, 2006).

message, "If you need help, call this number." It was the number to our recovery ministry. Soon, the clubs began to call and ask for more napkins. Many people go to clubs and bars seeking a moment of excitement to numb the gnawing pain of an empty life, and they often leap at the chance to have a serious conversation with someone about their problems. Still other members of our church went to hospitals, fire departments, apartment complexes, and nursing homes. We found out there are 30,000 refugees who live within ten miles of our church. They had been invisible to us. We had no idea they even existed.

When our people got out of the box, God used us to touch thousands of lives with His love.

The Bible tells us over and over to "remember." We need to remember that we were once outsiders, but God took us into His heart—not because we did enough to earn His love, but in spite of the fact that we didn't. We were enemies, without hope and with nothing to offer. If we remember the grace of God that rescued us, we'll be far more compassionate with others who are struggling and haven't yet felt God's loving touch. We also need to remember that He entrusted to us the enterprise of caring for the world. We are His voice, His hands, and His feet. He cares for people today through us.

Watch your heart. If you see prejudice, don't excuse or tolerate it. When you notice all the angry, divisive talk going on, don't join in. Open your eyes to see the outcasts around you, whether they are wearing rags or Italian suits and Gucci

Open your eyes to see the outcasts around you, whether they are wearing rags or Italian suits and Gucci shoes. Everyone needs God's touch.

shoes. Everyone needs God's touch. Don't insist that people meet some standard before you're willing to reach out to them. We might be convinced we have correct political views and right theology, but we may have wrong hearts. Today's Christians are known more for what we're against than what we're for. If we insist that people agree with us before we care for them, we'll have a very restricted circle of ministry.

What if we became known as people of love, justice, mercy, and humility? People may have different beliefs or sexual practices, they may talk funny or smell weird, or they may hold political views you oppose. Look beyond all those differences, and show love anyway. That's what Jesus did for you. Do the same for them.

THINK ABOUT IT...

1. What are some boundary markers people use to include some and exclude others? Which of those have you used?

2. Why do you think the Pharisees' religious bigotry was especially offensive to Jesus?

3. How did the Good Samaritan care for the man who had been robbed and beaten? What risks did he take? What sacrifices did he make? How do you think the Jewish leaders listening to the story felt about the message of this parable?

4. Read Ephesians 2:14-18. In what way is the death of Jesus the ultimate remedy for our feelings of superiority and our desire to exclude people?

5. Read Matthew 25:34-40. Who are "the least of these" in your world? What are some practical things you can do to care for them?

6. Does remembering the grace of God for you propel you to reach out to more people and care for them? Why or why not?

7. Who is a person down the street, in the next office, or under a bridge who could use a friend? What's your next step?

CHAPTER 7
TURN YOUR HEART TOWARD HOME

What women want: To be loved, to be lis-
tened to, to be desired, to be respected, to be
needed, to be trusted, and sometimes, just to
be held.

What men want: Tickets to the World Series.

—Dave Barry

More than anything, we long for meaningful family relationships. We
want to enjoy the love, laughter, and rich conversation we've seen in
the lives of a few families we admire. When high hopes are dashed,
however, the disappointment crushes us. There is perhaps no other
place where our desires collide so painfully with harsh reality.

Many families experience frequent and violent collisions between
spouses or between parents and kids—or both. In response, some
families explode. Others implode, which is just as bad . . . if not worse.
Instead of talking about the tension they feel, they bottle it up and try

to act as if nothing is wrong. Like a volcano, the family may appear placid for a while, but sooner or later the hot magma of resentment, hurt, and betrayal boils over and burns everyone.

We would like to think that Christians are exempt from family troubles. After all, we love Jesus, don't we? Yet when the Barna Group researched families in America, they found that divorce occurs in 33 percent of all couples, with the same percentage among the segment of born-again Christians who are not in evangelical churches. Among evangelical Christians, the divorce rate is only slightly better: 26 percent. Among Catholics, the figure is 28 percent. But strikingly, people who identify broadly with all Protestant churches get divorced at a higher rate than the national average: 34 percent.[27]

Of course, divorce is only the most visible and measurable statistic. It would be harder for studies to verify the unrelieved stress, unresolved conflict, and unhealed hurts within American families. Many couples that don't get divorced live in relationships that could be described as little more than an armed truce.

I didn't grow up in an antagonistic family environment—and for that I'm grateful. My parents have one of the most wonderful marriages I've ever seen. So did my grandparents, who were married for 72 years. At their 72nd anniversary party, my grandmother stood up and announced, "Ladies and gentlemen, I've finally decided to stay with this man!"

I used to take my parents' relationship for granted, but during the time when Kim and I dated and married, I began to see them through her

27 Barna Group, "New Marriage and Divorce Statistics Released," March 31, 2008, www.barna.org/barna-update/article/15-familykids/42-new-marriage-and-divorce-statistics-released

eyes. My dad is a leader in the church, and he's a leader in our family, but he's never authoritarian. We laugh, talk, and joke around, but he has earned our respect by his unquestioned integrity and courage. My mother is submissive to his leadership, but it's not because she's weak and easily controlled. Dad asks for Mom's input on virtually every major decision, and he seldom (if ever) moves forward until Mom has bought in to his ideas.

In public, Dad always gives Mom credit for how much she contributed to this event or that plan. They're not in competition with each other at all—ex-**They have deep mutual love and respect. They're best friends, which is a sure foundation for a great marriage.** cept in showing affection and honor. They have deep mutual love and respect. They're best friends, which is a sure foundation for a great marriage. In contrast, I've seen many couples that seem more like business partners or roommates than loving married couples.

Don't get me wrong. My parents didn't agree about everything. I'm sure they had plenty of heated discussions about all kinds of issues. Anytime two people are in a room, there are going to be at least three opinions: yours, mine, and ours. But Mom and Dad didn't argue in front of the kids. They had plenty of healthy discussions and debates in front of us, but when the needle passed the red line on the conflict-ometer, they left the room to hash things out. When they came back, the tension was gone. They had reached a mutual decision in a way that strengthened their relationship instead of tearing it apart.

Dad was very protective of my mom. If the boys were arguing with her, Dad often stepped in to referee. If one of us said, "Well, *she* said this and that!" Dad would look the offending boy in the eye and tell him plainly, "Son, show respect to your mother. Don't ever refer to her as 'she.' That's your mother you're talking about. Do you understand?"

But honesty went both ways. My parents were also willing to admit when they were wrong. I remember my father calling several family meetings to tell us, "I'm sorry. I disciplined you in a wrong way. I was angry and said things I shouldn't have said. I need to ask you to forgive me." A parent's admission of wrong clears away a lot of resentment. It goes a long way to create an atmosphere of truth, honor, and love.

Kim's parents are much like mine. Her mom and dad have also had a wonderful partnership. Her dad is the head of the house, but he always values and welcomes her mom's opinions and desires. Kim never remembers either of her parents speaking negatively in frustration about the other. They both worked full-time jobs and came home to a warm, loving, affirming spouse—no nagging, no blaming, no competition . . . just unconditional affection and acceptance.

Kim and I have tried to create a home modeled on the ones our parents gave us. We're committed to honor one another, communicate in healthy ways, and quickly resolve anything that comes between us. When God called me into the ministry, He didn't just call me—He called the two of us. Kim and I are a team, a partnership. Every couple needs this kind of commitment, no matter what careers they choose.

For both Kim and me, the lessons we learned were more caught than taught. We learned about loyalty and love by watching our parents live those qualities all day every day—not perfectly, but consistently. Solomon advised us, "Good friend, follow your father's good advice; don't wander off from your mother's teachings. Wrap yourself in them from head to foot; wear them like a scarf around your neck" (Proverbs

6:20-21, *The Message*). In some families, this advice is hard to follow. Our task—and our privilege—is to make it normal for our kids to soak up wisdom from both parents. The home is where kids are supposed to learn faithfulness, kindness, courage, and hope. They'll take away something from us to wear "around their necks"—either heartache and resentment, or love and loyalty. I'm going for the second set.

THE MYTH, THE BOND

If an alien landed on earth and observed only from media and advertisements how families function in America, what would he conclude? I think he would be led to believe that fiery hot passion must be the foundation of relationships. Without constant, intense emotion and acrobatic sexual exploits, a healthy marriage is impossible. I'm afraid that many of us believe the same myth.

Lust sells all kinds of products and brings in millions at movie box offices, but it's a lousy foundation for a loving, lasting marriage. Lust is about taking; it is entirely self-serving. Others are valuable only if they contribute to our security, significance, or happiness. When people fail in any way to give us what we want, they become expendable.

In contrast, love is marked by giving, not getting. Love delights in serving, building up, and making the most of the other person—not for selfish purposes, but for the good of the person. If we settle for lust, what happens when the passions cool? Some think it's perfectly acceptable to look for someone new to fan the flames, and others assume they'll have to settle for second best. Disappointment is a crumbling foundation for a relationship.

Couples walk down the aisle with fairytale expectations. They look into each other's eyes and think, *You're the person of my dreams. You complete me. You're going to make me supremely happy, secure, thrilled, and fulfilled. That's not too much to ask, is it?* When expectations are sky high, normal adjustments and struggles soon shatter the dream. If the husband and wife haven't seen parents who handled difficulty with grace and strength, they have few skills with which they can resolve their own troubles. They drift into separate worlds, protect themselves, blame each other, and create another generation of kids who grow up without learning life's lessons from their parents.

Without genuine love in a marriage, every disagreement can drive couples apart. Parents compete for the attention of the kids and try to get their needs met through **Comparison kills.** some other means: people, sports, work, drugs, shopping, or thrills. When love withers, our eyes look elsewhere. We may think *Desperate Housewives* is the template for future choices!

Comparison kills. Plenty of spouses tell one another, "I wish you could make as much money as Jim," or "It would sure help if you had a career like Sue." Parents compare their children to others in all kinds of categories: grades, sports, club involvement, etc. Negative comparisons make people feel small, and few comparisons of any kind have a positive effect. If a husband says, "You look a lot better than that woman," what's his wife going to think? She realizes he's checking out other women, and he's going to find some (maybe plenty) who are prettier! Instead of being affirmed, she feels threatened. Most comparisons can cut and wound deeply.

High hopes on a wedding day often devolve into bland, empty toleration. The relationship becomes little more than a business deal. He provides money, stability, and status. She provides childcare, sex, some prestige if she's a trophy wife, and maybe income if she has a career. In such an environment, the relationship with children gets tricky. Youngsters may be seen as annoyances that get in the way of a parent's upward climb, or a parent might devote all his or her (mostly her) energy and affection to the children—and sometimes, only one of several children. Sticky . . . very sticky.

In fact, some couples live like college roommates. They stay under the same roof but in different rooms. They divide the responsibilities around the house, and they may hold separate checking accounts. Behind the calm façade of "family" lurks deep heartache. They know marriage should be far more, but they have no idea how to make it work. They try to walk on eggshells so they won't crack the fragile ego of the other person, but it's more like walking in a minefield where explosions occur randomly and unexpectedly.

There's a better option for couples. In his letter to the Ephesians, Paul painted a beautiful picture of the power of the gospel to change hearts and provide purpose. Narrowing in on specifics (Ephesians 4:17—6:9), he described the importance of moment-by-moment choices to "put off" old, selfish habits and "put on" good and godly choices. He gave several examples of how to make this switch that involve honesty, possessions, language, forgiveness, and dealing with anger. Then he outlined how a transformed heart makes a difference in the most important relationships, including marriage and parenting. Near the end of his description of a Christ-centered marriage, he wrote, "Each of you also must love his wife as he loves himself, and the wife must respect her husband" (Ephesians 5:33). Love and respect. They're certainly related, but they're not the same.

In fact, I recommend a book titled *Love & Respect* by Emerson Eggerichs. The cover copy succinctly summarizes the theme:

> Psychological studies affirm it, and the Bible has been saying it for ages. Cracking the communication code between husband and wife involves understanding one thing: that unconditional respect is as powerful for him as unconditional love is for her. It's the secret to marriage that every couple seeks, and yet few couples ever find.[28]

Kids are sponges. They soak up every message—verbal and nonverbal—in their environments. The old saying still holds true: "The most important thing a parent can do for his kids is to love his spouse." Parents don't need to be perfect for children to thrive. Psychologist Virginia Satir said all that kids need is "good enough parents." But "good enough" always includes liberal amounts of affection, security, and affirmation.

Kids are sponges. They soak up every message—verbal and nonverbal—in their environments.

---

28   Emerson Eggerichs, *Love & Respect* (Nashville: Thomas Nelson, 2004), front flap.

Today's schoolchildren intermingle with plenty of kids from broken homes. The parents of many students have been married and divorced so many times they need a scorecard to keep up with step- and half-siblings. When Kim and I got married, we made a commitment: We would never utter the D-word in our home. We didn't want our kids (or us, for that matter) to ever think divorce was an option. We wanted them to know they could count on us to work things out no matter how hard life got.

I realize that some people reading this book will be divorced and struggling with singleness or blended family relationships. God is the God of second chances—third, fourth, and fifth chances too! Start where you are today and make a commitment to hang tough, to love no matter what, and to resolve any and all differences. Divorced people have deep wounds and scars, and blended families are often as complex as quantum physics. Don't despair, and don't give up. Make a choice to be faithful. You owe that to everyone involved.

Wounds and stress cause us to become self-protective and self-absorbed. Decades ago, farm life was hard and the mortality rate was high, but at least families spent a lot of time together. These days many couples see each other only a few minutes each day. Between work, taking kids to sports and other activities, entertainment, technology, and shopping, they pass like electrons in the night—near the speed of light. Parents spend only minutes with their children in a long, busy day, and the time is often devoted to checking on grades, finding out where they've been, or trying to break up fights—not exactly "quality time." The speed of life and mobility exhaust us, and the busyness of our schedules takes up most of our precious time. If we're not careful, we become disengaged roommates to our children, and they have to fend for themselves.

FROM DISAPPOINTMENT TO HONOR

No matter how much we feel hurt, no matter how far we've drifted from a spouse's heart, and no matter how high we've erected walls of self-protection, it's never too late to start over. God loves to change lives. He can bring light out of darkness and resurrect the dead to new life. If He can create the universe and raise Jesus from the tomb, He can resurrect a marriage and a family. A few principles give us clear direction.

First, fill the well.

A foundational principle of life is that we can't give away what we don't possess. We can't offer love, forgiveness, and wisdom to others if our well is dry. Many of us live like the line in the old Jackson Browne hit: "Running on empty, running blind. Running into the sun but I'm running behind."[29]

A foundational principle of life is that we can't give away what we don't possess.

We can't offer love, forgiveness, and wisdom to others if our well is dry.

We can't forgive unless we're first convinced God has forgiven us. We won't extend love to others until we experience the love of God that surpasses understanding (Ephesians 3:19). And we will never be able to warmly accept others as long as we feel unacceptable to God. The gospel of grace tells us that we're more valuable to God than all the gold, diamonds, oil, and real estate in the world. We were so wicked that it took the death of God's Son to pay for our sins, but He loves us so much He was willing to go to the cross to suffer and die for us.

---

29 "Running on Empty" © 1977, 1978 Swallow Turn Music.

As long as we see ourselves primarily as victims, we won't make much (or any) progress in healing our most important relationships. We have been wronged, but we have also wronged others. Our first step is to be ruthlessly honest about the emptiness and darkness in our own hearts so God can fill us with love and light.

Jesus explained, "A good man brings good things out of the good stored up in his heart, and an evil man brings evil things out of the evil stored up in his heart. For the mouth speaks what the heart is full of" (Luke 6:45). We need to fill our hearts with His grace.

Follow the law of reciprocity.

Paul assures us, "Do not be deceived: God cannot be mocked. A man reaps what he sows. Whoever sows to please their flesh, from the flesh will reap destruction; whoever sows to please the Spirit, from the Spirit will reap eternal life" (Galatians 6:7-8).

We don't have to look far to see how this principle works in our relationships. When I criticize someone harshly, what do I get back? The person usually reacts by blaming me and then raising the stakes with even more emotion . . . and I don't have to wait long for the reaction! But the opposite is also true. When I take time to encourage Kim or my kids genuinely and specifically, their eyes light up. I get warm hugs in return, and it opens the door for wonderful, relaxed conversations. They might even tell me they like my latest sermon. (It's rare, but it happens occasionally!)

The law of reciprocity has spiritual as well as physical results. However, those devoted to God's work can, with His help, also rely on the "law of the harvest": We reap *what* we sow, *more than* we sow, and *after* we sow.

Develop the skill to affirm people.

Some of us grew up in homes that thrived on authentic affirmation. No matter what happened, in success or failure, family members felt encouraged rather than berated. When a child or spouse had a big success, everyone celebrated like mad! No one got jealous. When someone experienced a painful disappointment, others came around with hugs and words of hope for the future.

People need to hear three messages, and they need to hear them consistently: (1) "I love you like crazy," (2) "I'm so proud of you," and, (3) "This is what I see in your future."

People need to hear three messages, and they need to hear them consistently: (1) "I love you like crazy," (2) "I'm so proud of you," and, (3) "This is what I see in your future." These statements, though, have to be more than empty, parroted words. We need to be specific about what we see in spouses or children that we're so proud of. We need wisdom to connect present abilities with future possibilities. And we need to think carefully and let genuine emotion flow from our hearts.

Actress Celeste Holm once observed, "We live by encouragement and die without it—slowly, sadly, angrily." Don't let people die around you.

Resolve conflict quickly.

The apostle Paul was a brilliant theologian and a courageous pioneer for the early church, but he also gave very practical advice. In his letter to the Ephesians, he quoted Psalm 4:4: "In your anger do not sin." Then he added, "Do not let the sun go down while you are still angry, and do not give the devil a foothold" (Ephesians 4:26-27). Humans are amazing creatures. We can turn the slightest offense into the most intractable bitterness. All it takes is neglect, a little time, and a good imagination. Before long the original, minor offense can morph into justification for World War III.

Bitterness is a poison, but it's one we gladly drink because it feels so right. After all, the person who hurt us deserves our resentment! Some of us live for years letting old hurts distort every motive and ruin every relationship. We love to think about getting the other person back, but we fail to realize how the failure to forgive affects us.

Pastor Frederick Buechner observed:

> Of the Seven Deadly Sins, anger is possibly the most fun. To lick your wounds, to smack your lips over grievances long past, to roll over your tongue the prospect of bitter confrontations still to come, to savor to the last toothsome morsel both the pain you are given and the pain you are giving back—in many ways it is a feast fit for a king. The chief drawback is that what you are wolfing down is yourself. The skeleton at the feast is you![30]

When we feel hurt, our natural reaction is fight or flight—we either lash back in anger or we run and hide. We need to find a radical, different way to respond: How about *talking*? We can ask the other person to clarify why he thinks and feels as he does. We can ask her to explain and help us understand. And here's a novel approach: While the person is talking, we can *listen* instead of planning a counterattack.

---

30   Frederick Buechner, *Wishful Thinking*, (San Francisco: Harper San Francisco, 1993), p. 2.

During such conversations, some misunderstandings might be cleared up fairly easily, yet genuine emotional damage may still exist. In most cases, both parties are at least partly at fault. When we have been offended, God wants us to take the initiative to forgive—whether or not the person is sorry or even admits the offense. We can't make the other person respond with grace and forgiveness, and we can't force him or her to become trustworthy. All we can do is take the steps God wants us to take to attempt to resolve the issue. If the person responds and reconciles, that's fantastic. If not, we grieve the loss, trust God even more, and keep attempting to build relationships of honesty, love, trust, and respect.

Of course, situations vary widely in the number and severity of painful events. In cases of physical and sexual abuse, the spouse and kids may need to leave to save their lives. The news presents regular horror stories about the devastating impact of domestic violence. Reconciliation may not happen until the end of a long process, and maybe not at all.

If we delay, we find excuses for not addressing them at all. Walls go up, love erodes, and the beauty of a warm, supportive family takes a serious blow. Don't wait.

Paul's point, however, is to deal with problems as they surface. If we delay, we find excuses for not addressing them at all. Walls go up, love erodes, and the beauty of a warm, supportive family takes a serious blow. Don't wait. Develop the courage and skill to resolve conflict as soon as possible.

Honor those you love.

If we enter marriage with an "out clause," we'll always wonder if this disagreement or that disappointment is enough to dissolve the relationship. The most important human relationship needs a stronger foundation, and God has provided one: It's a *covenant*. When we marry, we're not just saying "I do" to a bride or groom; we're making a solemn statement to Almighty God. We're telling Him, "God, I trust that you've led me into this relationship. You called me into it, and you'll see me through every difficulty." There's no out clause, no parachute, no Plan B.

I'm not saying divorce is never appropriate. The Scriptures provide some legitimate reasons for a couple to dissolve their marriage, including sexual infidelity. However, the divorce rate is far too high because people bail out for relatively trivial reasons. Even adultery can be forgiven and the marriage restored if the offending person is repentant and trust is gradually rebuilt.

When you consider marriage as a covenant, you see your spouse as God's gift, not just a hormone-induced choice. It certainly is different from the way marriage is depicted in sitcoms, but look at the quality of those relationships! Besides, isn't it more romantic to believe that God has put the two of you together? Your spouse is God's good gift to you, even when you disagree, and even when you feel hurt. With this perspective, you honor your spouse by staying in the conversation, resolving differences, and looking for good instead of finding fault.

Kim and I see each other as God's gifts. I honor her for her character, talents, beauty, and wisdom. She honors me in all kinds of ways. We have very honest private conversations, but she always supports me in front of the kids, in front of the church, and in front of her friends.

I never have to wonder if she has my back. This confidence forms a bedrock of trust between us—which then reinforces a healthy, intimate marriage.

Trust God for wisdom and courage.

Many couples have their marriages and kids on autopilot. They launched their ship at the wedding, and now they expect things to take care of themselves. It's interesting that those same people spend hours in the intricacies of their favorite hobbies, laboriously study computer programs or games, and take their cars in for regular inspections and repairs, but they don't take time to analyze their most important relationships.

When a friend is having a marriage problem or trouble with kids, standard advice is really rich: "Just go with your heart." Thanks a lot. That's like saying, "You can trust the most desperately wicked part of you to give you answers to your most pressing problems!" Surely we can do better than that.

We may sometimes feel isolated and hopeless in our families, but we're never alone. God is with us, and He promises to give us the wisdom we need—if only we'll ask Him in faith. James reminds us:

If any of you lacks wisdom, you should ask God, who gives generously to all without finding fault, and it will be given to you. But when you ask, you must believe and not doubt, because the one who doubts is like a wave of the sea, blown and tossed by the wind. That person should not expect to receive anything from the Lord (James 1:5-7).

Some of the questions we face are clearly answered in the Bible: Don't lie, cheat, steal, harbor bitterness, or commit adultery. Love your enemies, care for the poor, and be gentle and humble in all relationships.

But we need wisdom—the application of God's truth—when dealing with the gray areas of life, the situations when the answers aren't quite as clear. How do we handle normal stresses in life? What career choices should we make? What are our priorities in how we spend time and money? How do we raise teenagers? (Answering that one would take another book or two. I have one teenager and another one close behind!)

In all these areas, God promises to lead us, to give us insights, and to guide our steps, but there are no guarantees that things will work out just the way we want. In fact, we need to trust Him even more in the most complex relationships of life because there are so many variables.

In fact, we need to trust Him even more in the most complex relationships of life because there are so many variables.

I can tell how much I'm trusting God by the ratio between worry and thankfulness. There's nothing wrong with concern. We're naturally concerned about money, kids, health, career, friends, purpose, and so on. But worry is concern on steroids! Worry creates mental obsessions about a person or problem. We spend hours daydreaming about finding the perfect solution or escaping the pain, but the more we think about it, the less peace we have.

Gratitude is both a choice and a result. We choose to thank God for His wisdom, sovereignty, goodness, and power—even when we're in the middle of a difficult circumstance. As we see Him work, our hearts sing and we thank Him for His gracious provisions. I may not feel like thanking God when I face difficulties, but it's an act of faith that delights God. It shows I trust Him even in the darkness.

IT'S YOUR MOVE

Many spouses and parents feel completely overwhelmed. They've tried to manage stress and heartache for a long time, and it has worn them down. The early dreams have faded. All that's left is a grim resolve to make it through another day . . . and maybe the fantasy of finding someone else to provide what they really want.

Difficulties are a reality of life. We're fallen people who live with fallen spouses and kids in a fallen world. The question isn't, "How can I avoid problems so I can have a perfectly happy life?" That's a pipedream, and if we see ourselves primarily as victims, we stay stuck in the quicksand of despair. The more perceptive question is, "How can I trust God to use this difficulty for good for my life, my marriage, and my children?"

Problems are watersheds that push us to one side or the other: to deeper wisdom and love, or to distance and distrust. It's our move.

Problems are watersheds that push us to one side or the other: to deeper wisdom and love, or to distance and distrust. It's our move. God has given us the privilege and responsibility to make choices about our direction. One leads to life and hope; the other to prolonged, draining isolation and resentment. Difficulties aren't our enemies. We avoid them if possible, of course, but we can't escape them all. We need God's perspective so we respond with faith and hope.

Paul wrote the Christians in Rome that facing problems produces spiritual fruit. In fact, the anticipation of seeing God use difficulties to shape us and deepen us is a cause for celebration! He wrote:

There's more to come: We continue to shout our praise even when we're hemmed in with troubles, because we know how troubles can develop passionate patience in us, and how that patience in turn forges the tempered steel of virtue, keeping us alert for whatever God will do next. In alert expectancy such as this, we're never left feeling shortchanged. Quite the contrary—we can't round up enough containers to hold everything God generously pours into our lives through the Holy Spirit! (Romans 5:3-5, *The Message*)

A professor in Bible school told me that couples need to treat each other like a master gardener tends his flowers—with tenderness and skill. Left untended, a garden fills with weeds, becomes littered with limbs from storms, or is decimated by insects. An attentive gardener, though, notices the problems before they get out of hand and does whatever it takes to resolve them. He has an array of sprays, granules, compost, shears, and other tools, and he knows how to use them.

Paul told the Ephesian men, "Love your wives, just as Christ loved the church and gave himself up for her" (Ephesians 5:25). That's the standard of love and attention: the sacrifice of Jesus Christ on the cross. When we genuinely love our wives, we'll care for their needs as attentively as we care for our own. We will devote our energies and our resources to protect them, provide for them, and give their lives ultimate meaning. When women receive even a fraction of that degree of love, their hearts sing and they reciprocate by honoring their husbands—which, of course, causes their men to shower them with even more love. The cycle, though, doesn't end there. Another generation is watching. When kids see their parents loving and respecting each other, they want the same thing for themselves and usually have better discernment about choosing their own life partners.

It's easy to play the blame game, but accusations sour relationships. The first item of business isn't to get your spouse or kids to change— it's for you to change. When you step back and trust God to provide clear eyes to see yourself, you can be honest with Him about your sins and failures. God has to fill the well before you can draw from it. Then and only then will you find the inner strength and motivation to move toward your spouse and kids with a heart of love instead of blame.

The principles of love, forgiveness, respect, and honor apply to every family: classic nuclear families, single moms, young couples, empty nesters, blended families, widows and widowers, and those who are recently divorced or who have a string of divorces behind them. Present situations and past memories can haunt us. We need God's grace and power to transform us so we love unconditionally.

The process of change is always messy and difficult. No one promised that following Jesus would be easy. But it's worth it. When we put our lives in His hands and trust Him to change us from the inside out, He will show us how much He loves us, and He will revolutionize how we respond to those we love. It's a fight, but it's a glorious one you can win!

THINK ABOUT IT...

1. What are some differences between lust and love? Think of your favorite movies (especially chick flicks) and sitcoms. How are lust and love depicted?

2. Do you agree or disagree with the observation that women thrive on love and men on respect? Explain your answer.

3. When you were a kid, what did you soak up from your home environment? (Think of values, skills in conflict resolution, expressions of love and affirmation, etc.) How are those things being repeated in your family today?

4. What does "don't let the sun go down on your anger" mean in practice? How does delay give the devil an opportunity? What is he trying to accomplish?

5. How might God use problems in your marriage or with your kids to actually strengthen those relationships?

6. What's one thing you need to do to improve your family relationships?

CHAPTER 8
THE TRIGGER OF BLESSING

By living fully, recognizing that all we do is by His
power, we honor God; He in turn blesses us.

—Becky Laird

In 2005 when Kim and I were living out West, I was studying the Old
Testament book of Habakkuk. Things weren't going well for the prophet and God's people. A brutal enemy had overrun the country, and God
told them it was only going to get worse! But God hadn't given up on
His children. He told Habakkuk:

"Write down the revelation
    and make it plain on tablets
    so that a herald may run with it.
For the revelation awaits an appointed time;
    it speaks of the end
    and will not prove false.
Though it linger, wait for it;
    it will certainly come
    and will not delay" (Habakkuk 2:2-3).

The phrase "Write down the revelation" captured my attention. In 24-point font, I typed "DREAM BIG" at the top of a page. Then I prayed, "God, I want to dream without limits. Will you give me Your dreams? I'm not going to analyze things, and I'm not going to limit the revelation by reason, money, or my situation in life. I'm just going to ask Your Spirit to guide my thoughts. I'll type whatever You put on my heart." As I opened my heart to God, the Spirit impressed me with fifteen things to write down. I printed the list, folded the paper, and put it in a file.

THE RETURN

About two years later, I was rummaging through my files looking for some sermon notes, and I found the file folder with the list of dreams. I pulled it out, looked at it, and I thought, *That was so stupid. Why did I waste my time and paper on that pointless exercise?* I wadded up the list and threw it in the trash.

I didn't discard it because times were hard and I was discouraged. In fact, it was just the opposite. Kim and I finally had a sense of stability. We had some money to pay the bills, our kids were thriving, and my career was doing well. Even positive circumstances can reduce the size of your God-given dream. I wasn't hungry for the dream because I was satisfied with my life.

A few months later, Pastor George called and asked me to pray about coming back to Calvary. I wanted to know, "What role do you have in mind?"

He said only, "Ben, I just want you to pray. I need you to hear from God."

I couldn't imagine moving halfway across the country to a job without a title or set of responsibilities. Maybe I hadn't heard him right. I asked again, "Pastor George, what do you have in mind for me?"

As patiently as ever, he repeated, "I can't tell you. Just pray and ask God to speak to you."

Earlier in the church plant in the West, we had been through hell but had come out on the other side with greater wisdom and strength. God was working in the lives of our church and our family. Why in the world would I want to leave now? After Pastor George hung up, I called Kim to tell her about the offer. As we talked, I tried to rationalize all the reasons we shouldn't leave our current situation. Kim only replied, "Come home. I want to show you something."

When I got home, I saw a piece of paper sitting on the counter. It had been crumpled up, but someone had smoothed it out. I looked more closely: It was the paper I'd thrown away months before . . . the list of dreams God had put on my heart two years earlier. I picked it up and read it. The top three things on my dream list were:

It was the paper I'd thrown away months before . . . the list of dreams God had put on my heart two years earlier.

- That God would let me honor J. Don George in his latter years;

- That God would give me the opportunity to pastor alongside Pastor George at Calvary Church; and,

- That God would use me to build the church so that Pastor George would see the church grow far more than he'd seen before. It would be his lasting legacy.

I set the paper down and looked at Kim. I was flooded with emotions. A bit confused, I asked her how this paper had survived after I had thrown it away and forgotten about it months before.

She explained, "Ben, one day I saw this paper crumpled up in the trash. I took it out and read it, and it broke my heart. I knew God had put these dreams in your heart years ago, and I knew He wasn't finished yet. I couldn't stand the thought of you giving up, so I pulled those broken dreams out of the trash. I've kept this paper safely tucked away for the day God would revive them in you. Today is that day."

I'm so grateful for Kim.

It would seem that Pastor George's call and the message on the paper formed a direction that was crystal clear, yet it wasn't quite that simple. Kim and I prayed and wrestled with the decision for three long months. During all that time, Pastor George didn't tell me any more about the job he envisioned for me. He didn't want to muddy my motivational waters by dangling any incentives in front of me. He wanted my reasoning to be "pure and undefiled."

As we prayed and talked to people in our church, some were very supportive, but a few reacted in ways that shocked us. Maybe we shouldn't have been surprised, but we were. We had poured blood, sweat and tears into our ministry out West, and we were finally starting to see results. God was blessing, and we enjoyed see Him work in us and through us.

When we mentioned the possibility of leaving, some people in the church accused us of "taking the easy way out" if we went back to Texas. They had no clue. It would have been far easier to stay where we were. Others wondered out loud—in front of plenty of people—if we were going back because I had been promised a high-profile position. I tried to tell them Pastor George had made a point of *not* making any promises, but they didn't believe me. When they asked about the details of the role I had been offered, I told them, "I don't really know. If we go, it'll be on a word from God. Nothing else." They couldn't get their minds around the concept of submission without guarantees. Their suspicions continued to grow. We were trying very hard to hear from God, but His voice sometimes was drowned out by the cacophony of criticism and doubt from those who could have (and should have) supported us.

Finally, Kim and I sensed God's clear direction. I resigned from the church, and we packed up to move back to Texas. It was one of the hardest decisions we've ever made, but we were convinced it was God's design for us.

The trigger of God's blessing is honor.

In the five years since we've been back at Calvary, God has allowed me to live the dreams He put on my heart that day when I was studying Habakkuk, plus many more. The journey from the day we arrived back to Texas until now has been rocky, to say the least, but God has led us in powerful ways. I believe Pastor George feels honored by Kim and me, and he's getting to see his church blossom as never before. The key to it all isn't a list of church growth strategies, my preaching prowess (I wish), or luck.

The trigger of God's blessing is honor.

When I read Habakkuk years before, God put it on my heart to honor Him and Pastor George. No matter what happened, if God blew the doors off or if we struggled to grow, I was committed to honor God and my spiritual dad, Don George.

In the first months after we came back to Texas, I still had my doubts. If I expected God to make the way as smooth as silk, I was very disappointed. We had bought a nice house while in the western part of the country, but when we moved, the real estate market was tanking. For a year after we returned to Texas, our house sat empty. We had no buyers because there were no lookers. On top of that, we had a string of shady realtors, one of which even stole appliances from our vacant house. All that year, we lived in a little, unfurnished apartment . . . waiting and waiting. Most of our furniture, dishes, and other things were in storage. Was this really God's plan for our family?

Many times I concluded we had made a really stupid decision to come back. When the house finally sold, we didn't exactly celebrate because we had to pay tens of thousands of dollars at the closing. In spite of the loss, however, this moment was significant. As we signed the papers, we felt like Cortez when he led the Spanish invasion of Mexico: We were burning the ships and there was no turning back.

The next Sunday, I didn't want to preach. I was still feeling hurt, angry, and confused. I talked to Pastor George, and he told me to give it everything I had, no matter how I felt. After I preached in the first service, a man I'd never met came up to me. He had no idea what had happened the previous week, but God had whispered to him. He handed me an envelope and said, "Pastor Ben, I can imagine it's been hard moving all the way from out West. I want to help you and your family." I thanked him, and he walked away. I thought the envelope might contain a hundred dollars or so (for which I'm always thankful). But when I removed the check, it was for exactly the amount I'd had to take to our closing a few days before. I was overwhelmed and stunned . . . and very grateful. I think I preached the best I've ever preached in the next service!

In the years since we returned to Calvary, God has brought us people—staff and volunteers—with a passion to honor Him and Pastor George. The people I work with each day are like David's mighty men. We go to battle side by side, fighting for each other to advance God's kingdom. Sometimes we get bloody and dirty, but we defend each other no matter what. It's a beautiful thing to see. In fact, a man was sitting in church one Sunday when the Lord told him, "I want you to honor Ben Dailey the way you see him honoring Pastor George." He has become one of my most treasured staff members.

In addition, I've watched the Lord handpick a team of pastors and their wives who serve alongside me with fierce tenacity and honor—men like Jeremy Mount, Chris Ayon, Rick Botello, Elmer Canas, Andrew Jacobson, Stacey Blackmon, and Kirtis Langlais. I could keep listing names, and in all honesty, I could fill the pages of another book with stories about our pastoral staff, their wives, and countless servant leaders whom I consider priceless. I am often reminded of the moments Kim and I committed to honor the people God put over us in hope of creating a culture of honor on our own team in the future. Today, that desire has been realized.

The people I work with each day are like David's mighty men. We go to battle side by side, fighting for each other to advance God's kingdom.

HONOR AND BLESSING

The Gospel of Mark describes a time when Jesus went back to His hometown. As He spoke in the synagogue, the people were amazed, yet afterward a number of skeptics voiced their views. Sure, Jesus was preaching more powerfully than anyone had ever heard before, and He was healing people, but wasn't He just Mary's boy? He couldn't possibly be the Messiah!

Hearing their doubts must have hurt Jesus. He was pouring out His heart to them, and soon He would pour out His life on the cross. Yet they were unwilling to receive Him or His message. Mark describes His response:

> Jesus said to them, "A prophet is not without honor except in his own town, among his relatives and in his own home." He could not do any miracles there, except lay his hands on a few sick people and heal them. He was amazed at their lack of faith (Mark 6:4-6).

Because the people refused to honor Him, Jesus could only work a few miracles—nothing like what He wanted to do. Scripture doesn't say He "would not" heal the sick, restore sight to the blind, cast out demons, and raise the dead; it says he "could not." The people's lack of faith and their unwillingness to honor Him effectively tied His hands.

The trigger of blessing applies in every relationship. When we honor a spouse, great things happen in a marriage. When we honor our children, they grow up with the two essentials every kid needs: roots and wings. When we honor our leaders, we set them free to trust God even more. When we honor our employers, we show respect for authority and earn their trust. Every sphere of our lives runs far better when it's oiled with honor.

I'm sure many people reading these words are disgusted and want to scream, "The person I have in mind doesn't deserve to be honored! You have no idea what a jerk he (or she) is!" I understand completely. It has been a lot easier to honor my dad or Don George than other leaders I've served under. Some people are full of undeniable integrity, kindness, and spiritual power. Others are full of suspicion, double-mindedness, and disloyalty.

It shouldn't matter. We honor people by treating them the way God treats them: with a powerful blend of truth and grace. We focus on the good, overlook trivial annoyances, and do our best to resolve genuine problems. When we honor difficult people, we don't passively let them abuse us or misuse us, but neither do we lash out in rage. We let go of bitterness, speak words that build instead of destroy, and work to build bridges of trust. No one says it is easy, but it's essential.

> We honor people by treating them the way God treats them: with a powerful blend of truth and grace. We focus on the good, overlook trivial annoyances, and do our best to resolve genuine problems.

Our culture has lost its sense of honor. I've heard some leaders point to the Watergate debacle as the turning point. Before the Senate hearings and Nixon's resignation, people had a higher view of authority. After that moment in history, we became suspicious of anyone in leadership. In fact, many movies and television shows are fiercely cynical about anyone in authority. But skepticism and hopelessness don't have to continue. It's up to believers to change the culture—at least our segment of it.

Honoring God

We honor God because He deserves every ounce of respect, love, and loyalty we can muster. He is the sovereign creator of the universe, the one who spoke and the galaxies were placed in the skies. But His immense power is only half of the story. He is also the tender shepherd who stepped out of the glory of heaven to live with us and die for us. He proved Himself beyond the shadow of a doubt.

It's good and right to worship God. The word *worship* is derived from the old English term "worthship." God is supremely worthy of our affection and obedience, our praise and our sacrifice.

When we honor God, we devote ourselves to Him and His cause without demanding payback or guarantees. Many of us trust God only because we expect to get blessings from Him. Certainly, He blesses us more than we deserve, but that's the point: We don't deserve it! If we're in it only to pad our résumé or gain pleasure or wealth, we'll be crushed when we go through inevitable dark times. But if we learn to honor God, no matter what comes, we find we can please Him just as well in the darkness as in the light.

But if we learn to honor God, no matter what comes, we find we can please Him just as well in the darkness as in the light.

One of the greatest movies of all time is *Chariots of Fire*, the story of two Olympic athletes. Harold Abrams ran in the 1924 Paris Olympic Games for self-glory. Every race was an opportunity to prove his reputation in victory or be shattered by failure. A Scottish runner, Eric Liddell, ran for the glory of God. When he learned that a qualifying heat for his event was scheduled for Sunday, he shocked the sports world by pulling out of the race. He refused to race "on the Lord's day." British officials tried to pressure him to put king and country above his spiritual convictions, but he refused. Half the nation was outraged; the other half admired his courage. Another runner gave Liddell his spot in a different event, one the Scot had never run before. He accepted the offer. As Liddell stood at the starting line, an American runner named Jackson Schultz handed him a scrap of paper. Shultz quoted a passage from 1 Samuel, and he had written a word of encouragement: "In the Old Book it says, 'He that honors me I will honor.' Wishing you the best of success always."

A few seconds later, the starter fired his gun. Still clutching the paper in his hand, Liddell rounded the track and won the race. For England? Yes, but even more, for God. Because Eric Liddell chose to honor God in the face of withering public criticism and official pressure, God honored him with a victory on the track.

Honor people

When I talk about honor being the trigger of blessing in every relationship, some people respond, "Well, Ben, I'd be glad to honor that person, but he doesn't honor me! When he honors me, I'll honor him . . . but not before." This misses the whole point.

In His most famous sermon, Jesus said:

> "If you love those who love you, what reward will you get? Are not even the tax collectors doing that? And if you greet only your own people, what are you doing more than others? Do not even pagans do that?" (Matthew 5:46-47)

As believers, we have the Spirit of God. We have the teaching of the Scriptures. We have the example of Jesus who loved, served, gave, and honored us with His presence when we didn't deserve it at all. Can't we do better than the tit-for-tat relationships of the pagans?

Peter wrote to believers who had been driven out of Jerusalem by persecution. They had every reason to feel sorry for themselves and turn the guns of blame on others. But Peter wrote, "Show proper respect to everyone, love the family of believers, fear God, honor the emperor" (1 Peter 2:17).

Our *natural* inclination is to crave honor for ourselves, but our *supernatural* inclination is to honor others more than ourselves.

Respect and honor are synonymous. In their hardship, Peter told the early Christians to honor everyone, from the most bedraggled refugee running for his life to the emperor who led the attacks. Similarly, Paul wrote the Romans, "Be devoted to one another in love. Honor one another above yourselves. Never be lacking in zeal, but keep your spiritual fervor, serving the Lord" (Romans 12:10-11).

Our *natural* inclination is to crave honor for ourselves, but our *supernatural* inclination is to honor others more than ourselves. Showing honor for those around us is a mark of the Spirit's work in our hearts.

THE FIGHT TO HONOR

We need to purge certain words from our mental vocabulary: "if," "if only," and "when." The conditions we set that prevent us from honoring other people short-circuit God's power and blessing in our lives. We may not clearly articulate such feelings, but they are reinforced loudly and clearly in our hearts: "I'll honor him if he's nice to me." "I'll show respect if only she gives me what I want from her." "I'll be delighted in my spouse, kids, boss, coworkers, neighbors, parents, or friends when I feel like it."

Too often, we get mixed up about feelings and obedience. When we don't feel like loving someone, we don't act in loving ways. When we don't have respect for someone in authority, we complain and gossip. If we go against our feelings, we believe we're being inauthentic—and we can't have that!

We need to put the horse before the cart. In order to honor others, the will must precede the emotions. We first choose to obey God, live for Him, and do the right thing whether we feel like it or not. Where would we be today if Jesus had given in to His emotions in the garden before He was arrested? He didn't want to go to the cross. He knew He would suffer excruciating physical pain, but that level of hurt was nothing compared to the spiritual abandonment He would experience by being separated—for the first and only time in eternity—from the Father in order to bear our sins on the cross.

We can make one of two mistakes, or maybe both. We can start in the wrong direction, expecting God to jump through our hoops, to fulfill our agendas, and to make us happy, successful, and popular. Some people who read these words will recoil and respond, "I don't do that!" Maybe not, but a spirit of entitlement saturates our culture—not just in regard to welfare and government handouts, but for the happiness and peace we think we deserve from God. How can we tell what's in our hearts? If we get upset every time something doesn't go our way, we can be sure we don't really understand the way of the cross. Real faith is holding blessings in one hand and suffering in the other, and trusting God to use both to accomplish His will.

The second mistake is giving up too soon. When we're in the crucible of being stretched by God, it's uncomfortable. We may hang in there for a while, but eventually get to the point where we seriously consider giving up. At those times we need a fresh infusion of courage, insight, and hope. When Kim and I returned to Texas, we came to that point many times, but we kept going back to the crumpled piece of paper. We were sure God had called us, and we refused to let go of His hand.

At those times we need a fresh infusion of courage, insight, and hope.

Sometimes I let difficult people and wounded hearts throw me off track. When I threw my dream list in the trash, I was making a choice to take the easy way. At that point, I was letting success and ease draw me away from God's best. But God wouldn't let me go. He reminded me of those dreams, and He reinforced them over and over again. It has been a fight, and until I die, it will continue to be a struggle. But I'm committed to honor Him no matter what.

THE PROMISE

The concept of honor brings us back full circle to our starting point. The commitment to honor God opens our hearts so we know Him more intimately and trust Him more fully. We delight in the Lord, and He gives us the desires of our hearts. Delighting in Him rivets our affections on Him. We understand grace more deeply, and we praise the excellencies of His character with joy and passion. Gradually, the things that matter to Him matter more to us. The things that grieve Him cause us to be sad, too. The things that thrill Him multiply our delight. In our commitment to honor God, He promises to give us an abundant life.

Jesus explained that our obedience opens the door to fabulous spiritual riches. On the night He was betrayed, He told His men, "Whoever has my commands and keeps them is the one who loves me. The one who loves me will be loved by my Father, and I too will love them and show myself to them" (John 14:21).

Isn't that what our hearts long for: to experience the love and presence of God? That's His promise to those who choose to honor Him above all other pursuits.

In both the Old and New Testaments, we find a command that includes a promise. Paul wrote: "Children, obey your parents in the Lord, for this is right. 'Honor your father and mother'—which is the first commandment with a promise—'so that it may go well with you and that you may enjoy long life on the earth'" (Ephesians 6:1-3).

Although written specifically about children and their parents, the promise also applies to our relationship with our heavenly Father. When we make the choice to honor Him, God opens the floodgates of heaven to bless us. We may not become rich, gorgeous, or famous—but those often turn out to be curses instead of blessings. Instead, we experience love, we gain wisdom, and we see God use us to change people's lives. Increasingly, our dreams and desires align with His heart. A rich, full, abundant life isn't problem-free, but we have the assurance that God will use every circumstance to accomplish His divine purposes. We can rest in that promise.

UP, OUT, AND DOWN

You don't have to go to a training class to begin a lifestyle of honor. You can do it now and always. We honor God by recognizing He is "far above all" and "as close as our breath." The beauty, magnitude, and order of creation shout about God's magnificence, and the Bible articulates the specifics of His character, will, and ways.

We honor leaders by understanding the burden they carry and supporting them with sincere appreciation and a helping hand. We can encourage others to honor them, too.

We honor those around us by speaking words of affirmation instead of ridicule. We find the good in them instead of harping on their faults. When they see the change in us, they may faint in disbelief, but when they get off the floor we can begin a new and better relationship.

We honor those below us on the pecking order—children and employees—by valuing them as people God loves. We notice their strengths, overlook petty issues, and cast a vision for their future.

And we honor the poor by reaching out to them with genuine love. We don't patronize them. Instead, we treat "the least of these" as if they represent Jesus . . . because they do. The Bible directs us to care for orphans and widows, but other categories of needy people today include single moms, refugees, and immigrants.

What can we expect when we choose a life of honor? Some of our friends and family members may think we're nuts, but we can be sure God will honor us.

What can we expect when we choose a life of honor? Some of our friends and family members may think we're nuts, but we can be sure God will honor us. The writer to the Hebrews said, "And without faith it is impossible to please God, because anyone who comes to him must believe that he exists and that he rewards those who earnestly seek him" (Hebrews 11:6).

When a farmer plants seeds, he expects a harvest. He won't detect any growth for a while, but it will come. In the same way, when we plant seeds of faith, hope, and love, God will give us a harvest of blessings in all our relationships. Of course, just as farmers have to battle weeds, droughts, and storms, we have our own battles. If we persevere, God's blessings will flow. Children naturally expect good things from their parents, and God is the ultimate parent! Jesus made the connection when He explained:

> "Which of you, if your son asks for bread, will give him a stone? Or if he asks for a fish, will give him a snake? If you, then, though you are evil, know how to give good gifts to your children, how much more will your Father in heaven give good gifts to those who ask him!" (Matthew 7:9-11)

God begins the cycle of blessing with unconditional grace. When we respond in faith and choose to love and honor Him, He doubles down the blessings in our lives. Then, of course, we love Him even more, and the cycle continues.

DREAM BIG

Honoring people is more than a feeling. It takes action. When we saw the needs of single mothers in our community, we went all out to provide for them. Over 2,000 of them responded to our invitation. We prepared a lavish banquet, gave their kids haircuts and nice gifts, paid some overdue bills, washed cars, and did all kinds of other things for them. When a family in our church found out a single mom had a special needs child and was without transportation, they bought her a brand new car.

Our men washed cars and checked air pressure in the tires. Some of the women stayed in line until midnight to have their tires checked. (There may have been some ulterior motives, though. I had told them some of the men helping that night were single. You should have seen the looks in those women's eyes!)

I can't tell you who benefited more from this event. Certainly, the single moms and their kids felt loved. They received tangible gifts and services, but they also appreciated the messages of value and honor. The people in our church got as much or more from the experience.

When we reach out to care for the disadvantaged, we tap into God's heart. We sense His compassion, and we realize the cost of giving and serving—a cost we're thrilled to bear. Kim observed that dreaming big to care for others is "the great equalizer." Suddenly, those we've held at a distance become real people with hopes and fears. The mothers who came for help love their children just as much as the mothers from wealthy suburbs, even if they don't have as many resources. When we realize how much our generosity can change lives, we see our possessions in a different light. How can we lavish more stuff on ourselves when some of God's choice people—people we now love—are going without? Dreaming big to care for others changes everything.

> **When we reach out to care for the disadvantaged, we tap into God's heart. We sense His compassion, and we realize the cost of giving and serving—a cost we're thrilled to bear.**

We didn't differentiate between "deserving" mothers and those who had ruined their marriages by dumb choices. We loved them all the same. We opened our arms and welcomed every mom who wanted to come: Christians and Muslims, Hispanics and whites, young and old. It was a big dream, and everybody was blessed. Over and over again, those dear ladies told us they had never felt so loved and honored in their lives. What a thrill for us! We received dozens of letters, notes, and calls thanking us. Some said they had been single moms for many years, and this event was the first time they had sensed God's kindness. Others shared a litany of heartaches they'd faced in the past year. Our church's care means the world to them.

The people providing all the gifts and services felt honored to be part of something so wonderful. We dreamed big, and God showed up.

After the event was over, we were exhausted, but in the best kind of way. We knew we had made a difference. As I thought about the night, I realized every person in our church had been completely devoted to reach out to these moms and their kids. We didn't have time to argue about doctrinal differences or worship music, and we didn't have the energy for jealousy and petty squabbles. We were all captured by God's heart for those people. Honoring the women and their children galvanized our unity and purpose.

Let me recommend a course of action that may seem counterintuitive. A few of us thrive on risks, but most people avoid any chance of failure, chaos, or loss. An authentic life of faith necessarily includes a measure of risk. Jesus Christ didn't just risk His *reputation* by coming to earth to live and suffer ridicule and rejection. He risked His *life*—and He paid the ultimate price. As our hearts are filled with the love, power, and grace of God, we want to imitate Him. We don't have to go to the same cross He hung on, but He wants us to dream big and give everything we've got . . . first to Him, and then to those around us. That's how we honor Him.

You may be thinking, *Ben, you don't know me. You don't know where I've been or what I've done. God can't use somebody like me. Maybe other people, but not me.*

Wrong. God used deceivers like Jacob, prostitutes like Rahab, perpetually clueless people like the disciples, and a kidnapper and murderer like Paul. If He's willing to forgive them, equip them, and direct them to make a difference for His kingdom, no one is off limits for His grace. He uses our sins to show us how much He is willing to forgive, and He uses our pain to give us empathy for others who are hurting. God doesn't demand perfection. He's looking for people who are open to His heart. When we take His hand day by day, God does things in us and through us that can't be explained except by the wonder and power of the Holy Spirit. That's what Paul meant when he prayed, "God can do anything, you know—far more than you could ever imagine or guess or request in your wildest dreams! He does it not by pushing us around but by working within us, his Spirit deeply and gently within us" (Ephesians 3:20, *The Message*).

The power of the Spirit is unleashed in us when we delight ourselves in the Lord and let Him transform the desires of our hearts.

The power of the Spirit is unleashed in us when we delight ourselves in the Lord and let Him transform the desires of our hearts. As fruit ripens on the tree, our passion to honor God grows gradually, almost imperceptibly, but it's the real thing. And as this passion grows, we experience plenty of collisions. That's how change happens. When we pray, read the Word, and interact with people, God reveals selfish motives, bad attitudes, and destructive habits—things we've tolerated for years. Suddenly, we have a choice: to close our eyes and keep going in the same direction, or accept the new perception and make radical, new decisions to please the One who rescued us. It's not a smooth, easy path. Those who long to honor God with all their might walk a rocky road, but it's worth it. God is thrilled when we courageously face each collision.

Fear, doubt, passivity, and half-hearted efforts are dream killers. They promise to eliminate our hearts' collisions with God, but they erode our spiritual strength. Fight against them. Cling to God's heart, and hang on.

Are you willing to dream big? Take some time now (or soon) to be alone. Open your mind and heart to the Spirit of God, and ask Him to give you dreams for the future. Ask, "Lord, what can I do to honor you? If there were no reservations, how would you want to use me? Give me Your dreams, Lord. Give me Your dreams." Sit quietly, and write down the things that come to mind.

Quite often, God uses our deepest heartache as our most valuable resource in touching lives. An incredible woman in our church had a baby who died tragically, and she later started a ministry to sit with other mothers who had lost babies. She doesn't ramble on with a bunch of Christian clichés or shallow sentiments; she just hugs the hurting women and sits in silence to begin to mend broken hearts.[31]

As you make your list, some dreams may come to mind quickly, but others surface only after a period of time. Don't hurry. A few of them (perhaps more than a few) may seem ridiculous, but write them down anyway. When you sense the Spirit is done, put the paper in a safe place. The Lord may draw your attention back to it months or years later, even after you've forgotten about it. Or you may want to look at it every year to see how God is fulfilling the dreams He put on your heart. Don't throw it away like I did. Sadly, many people throw their

---

31 For more information about this ministry, go to Mommies Enduring Neonatal Death, MEND.org.

dreams away. Some give up because life is so difficult they can't imagine God ever fulfilling their dreams out of such chaos. Others discard their dreams because life settles into a comfortable routine.

Get ready. As your desires collide with God's heart, it may feel like your world is coming to an end. But this collision is just the beginning!

I'm still working on the list God gave me years ago. I'm living the first three items today, but some are yet to come. I'm not worried, and I'm not in a hurry. It's about God's honor and God's timing, not mine.

Get ready. As your desires collide with God's heart, it may feel like your world is coming to an end. But this collision is just the beginning!

DREAM BIG

Open your heart and ask God to give you His dreams for your life.

_____

_____

_____

_____

_____

_____

_____

_____

_____

_____

_____

_____

_____

THINK ABOUT IT...

1.   Have you ever felt that God put a dream or a vision into your heart? What happened? Has it been fulfilled yet? Have you given up, or are you still waiting?

2.   Read Mark 6:4-6. The people in Jesus' hometown refused to honor Him. What were the results?

3.   What are some motivations to honor God? Which of them inspire you to love Him and trust Him more? Explain your answer.

4. Read 1 Peter 2:17. Is honoring people reserved for those we think deserve to be honored? Why or why not? Who are some people you can honor? What words can you speak and what actions can you take to honor them?

5. The main principle of this chapter is that honor is the trigger of blessing. Do you agree or disagree? Explain your answer.

6. What can we expect when we make choices to honor God and people? What does God promise? What are some difficulties we may face?

7.   If you haven't done it already, take some time to dream big.

8.   What are the two or three most important things you've learned
     from this book? When and how will you apply them?

ABOUT THE AUTHOR

Ben Dailey serves as the Lead
Pastor of Calvary Church,
a multi-site church in the
Dallas/Fort Worth Metro-
plex. Known for his creative
style of communication and
passion for non-conventional
ministry, he reaches one of
the most culturally diverse
congregations in the nation.
His unique ministry approach,
along with his passion to
reach the un-churched, has

produced an atmosphere for record growth. Ben has served as a church
planter and ministry consultant.

Ben grew up on the coast of central California. After graduating from
high school, he planned to go to college in Los Angeles. He was excited
about the bright lights, beautiful people, and fast living . . . but God
had other plans. Late one night, God met him and turned him around.
In an instant, God charted a new direction for Ben's life.

Ben's character, passions, values, and ministry philosophy have been shaped by the powerful influence of two men: his father and Pastor Don George. Ben's dad has been a consistent model of joyful sacrifice. Ben recalls that his parents always seemed to have needy strangers— such as drug addicts, unwed mothers, and homeless people—living in their home. Reaching out to the disadvantaged was normal in their family. But for Ben's dad, it was never merely duty. He delighted in caring for those who were overlooked by society.

Early in Ben's ministry, he met Pastor Don George at Calvary Church in Irving, Texas. Ben didn't know it at the time, but God had put it in Pastor George's heart to bring Ben and Kim under his care. Ben became his assistant, and Pastor George mentored him in every aspect of pastoral ministry. Ben saw him in every conceivable situation in serving God, church members, the community, and pastors of other churches. Pastor George's influence profoundly shaped Ben's heart and his career.

After Ben served as a pastor for several years in another city, Pastor George asked him to pray about coming back to Calvary Church. In the years since his return, Ben has led the church to reach out far beyond its then-existing membership. The church has become known for ethnic diversity, wide-ranging ministries to the poor, and powerful outreach to the lost. In these years, the church has seen phenomenal growth.

Ben has been married to his wife, Kim, for nineteen years. They have two children, Kyla and Kade.

USING *COLLIDE* IN CLASSES AND GROUPS

This book is designed for individual study, small groups, and classes. The best way to absorb and apply these principles is for each person to individually study and answer the questions at the end of each chapter then to discuss them in either a class or a group environment.

Each chapter's questions are designed to promote reflection, application, and discussion. Order enough copies of the book for everyone to have a copy. For couples, encourage both to have their own book so they can record their individual reflections.

A recommended schedule for a small group or class might be:

WEEK 1

Introduce the material. As a group leader, tell your story, share your hopes for the group, and provide books for each person. Encourage people to read the assigned chapter each week and answer the questions.

WEEKS 2–9

Each week, introduce the topic for the week and share a story of how God has used the principles in your life. In small groups, lead people through a discussion of the questions at the end of the chapter. In classes, teach the principles in each chapter, use personal illustrations, and invite discussion.

PERSONALIZE EACH LESSON

Don't feel pressured to cover every question in your group discussions. Pick out three or four that had the biggest impact on you, and focus on those, or ask people in the group to share their responses to the questions that meant the most to them that week.

Make sure you personalize the principles and applications. At least once in each group meeting, add your own story to illustrate a particular point.

Make the Scriptures come alive. Far too often, we read the Bible like it's a phone book, with little or no emotion. Paint a vivid picture for people. Provide insights about the context of people's encounters with God, and help people in your class or group sense the emotions of specific people in each scene.

FOCUS ON APPLICATION

The questions at the end of each chapter and your encouragement to group members to be authentic will help your group take big steps to apply the principles they're learning. Share how you are applying the principles in particular chapters each week, and encourage them to take steps of growth, too.

THREE TYPES OF QUESTIONS

If you have led groups for a few years, you already understand the importance of using open questions to stimulate discussion. Three types of questions are *limiting, leading,* and *open.* Many of the questions at the end of each lesson are open questions.

Limiting questions focus on an obvious answer, such as, "What does Jesus call himself in John 10:11?" These don't stimulate reflection or discussion. If you want to use questions like this, follow them with thought-provoking, open questions.

Leading questions require the listener to guess what the leader has in mind, such as, "Why did Jesus use the metaphor of a shepherd in John 10?" (He was probably alluding to a passage in Ezekiel, but many people don't know that.) The teacher who asks a leading question has a definite answer in mind. Instead of asking this kind of question, you should just teach the point and perhaps ask an open question about the point you have made.

Open questions usually don't have right or wrong answers. They stimulate thinking, and they are far less threatening because the person answering doesn't risk ridicule for being wrong. These questions often begin with "Why do you think . . . ?" or "What are some reasons that . . . ?" or "How would you have felt in that situation?"

PREPARATION

As you prepare to teach this material in a group or class, consider these steps:

Carefully and thoughtfully read the book. Make notes, highlight key sections, quotes, or stories, and complete the reflection section at the end of each chapter. This will familiarize you with the entire scope of the content.

As you prepare for each week's class or group, read the corresponding chapter again and make additional notes.

Tailor the amount of content to the time allotted. You won't have time to cover all the questions, so pick the ones that are most pertinent.

Add your own stories to personalize the message and add impact.

Before and during your preparation, ask God to give you wisdom, clarity, and power. Trust Him to use your group to change people's lives.

Most people will get far more out of the group if they read the chapter and complete the reflection each week. Order books before the group or class begins or after the first week

TO ORDER MORE COPIES

To order more copies of this book, go to www.influenceresources.com